# One hundred thing to do at Disneyland before you die

THE ULTIMATE BUCKET LIST DISNEYLAND AND
DISNEY CALIFORNIA ADVENTURE EDITION

CATHERINE F. OLEN

One Hundred Things to do at Disneyland before you die
The ultimate bucket list for Disneyland
and Disney California Adventure

© 2020 Catherine Olen

All Rights Reserved. No Portion of this book may be reproduced, stored in a retrieval system, or transmitted in any form or by any means—electronic, mechanical, photocopy, recording, scanning or other—except for brief quotations in critical reviews or articles, without the prior written permission of the publisher. Subject to permission under section 107 and/or 108 of the 1976 United States Copyright act. Requests for permission should be addressed to the publisher wwww.mousehangover.com. 949-234-7332

First paperback edition April 2020
ISBN 978-1-64822-006-7 (paperback)
ISBN 978-1-64822-007-4 (eBook)

Published by Mouse Hangover
www.Mousehangover.com

Please note: Every effort has been made to ensure the accuracy of information throughout this book. The information is believed to be accurate at the time of printing. The publish and author are not responsible for errors or omissions, for changes to details or the consequences of the readers reliance to the information provided. Attraction closures or updates are not the responsibility of the publisher or author and cannot be guaranteed at the time of use of this book.

Readers are welcome to contact the publisher for comments, updates or questions.

# About the Author

Catherine Olen has been visiting Disney parks since she was a small child. Olen fell in love with the parks built through the imagination of Walt Disney and became an annual passholder in 1991 and has held an annual pass ever since.

With each visit to the Disneyland resort, Olen has watched the theme parks change and grow throughout the years, and now, shares her love with people all over the world through her many books.

Olen continues to find renewed joy with each year as Disneyland brings new shows and attractions to the parks.

# Come Check Us Out

Check out new books, video and news at
www.Mousehangover.com
Subscribe to Mouse Hangover
Instagram—@TheMouseHangover
Twitter—@Mousehangover
Facebook—@Mousehangover
@WDWScavengerHunt

YouTube—Mouse Hangover

Other books:


The Ultimate bucket list
The Great Universal Studios Hollywood Scavenger Hunt
The Great Walt Disney World Scavenger Hunt

# Dedication

This book is dedicated to the millions of people who find Magic and Wonder within the gates of Disneyland.

To Walt Disney, the dreamer who saw a place where parents and children could play together.

To everyone whose unconditional love and support made this journey possible, I love you all!

# Table of Contents

Introduction ................................................................. xi
Before you enter Disneyland .......................................... 1

Disneyland ..................................................................... 9
   Main Street ............................................................... 11
   Hub ........................................................................... 43
   Fantasyland .............................................................. 45
   Toontown ................................................................. 69
   Star Wars: Galaxy's Edge ........................................ 83
   Frontierland ........................................................... 101
   Adventureland ....................................................... 111
   New Orleans Square ............................................. 120
   Critter Country ..................................................... 138
   Tomorrowland ....................................................... 144

Holidays at Disneyland ............................................... 151
   Halloweentime ...................................................... 153
   Christmastime at Disneyland ............................... 160

Disney California Adventure ....................................... 165
   Introduction .......................................................... 167
   Buena Vista Street ................................................. 169
   Hollywood Land .................................................... 176

| | |
|---|---|
| Grizzly Peak | 186 |
| Cars land | 192 |
| Pacific Wharf | 199 |
| Paradise Garden Park | 203 |
| Pixar Pier | 207 |
| Halloween | 215 |
| Christmas at Disney California Adventure | 222 |

# Introduction

From the grand opening on July 17, 1955, Disneyland has held the public captivated with a magic that is indescribable.

For years before Walt Disney ever conceived of this magical place, he was entertaining audiences with his adorable short subject cartoons starring his animated partner, Mickey Mouse.

Soon, Disney's ambition grew, creating full length motion pictures of the fairy tales he had heard growing up. Year after year, new characters danced on the silver screen as audiences fell in love again and again with Walt Disney's elaborate animated films.

As with everything in Disney's life, he would push the boundaries once again when he imagined a place where parents and children could play together. He wanted the families to interact as one, giving them memories that would last long after their children grew to adulthood.

Disneyland was the culmination of Disney's ambition. Starting with nothing more than an orange grove in Anaheim, California, Disney paced out the vision in his mind, literally walking the property as he developed the different lands. Seeing the park in his mind, as if it were already in existence, fueled his passion for the project and he led the team from ground breaking to completion in almost one year.

Walt Disney brought the animated films to life, putting the guest in the center of the action. Every person that walked across the drawbridge of Sleeping Beauty Castle was transported to the lands they saw at their local theaters. Children flew with Dumbo, rode the tea cups at the Mad Tea Party and traveled to Neverland to fight with Captain Hook. Throughout Fantasyland, guests could experience the stories in a myriad of different ways, sometimes on a boat, or flying through the air or even riding a caterpillar along larger than life leaves.

Tomorrowland offered wonders only seen in the pages of comic books or science fiction films. Traveling to inner space, flying to the moon or riding atop a flying saucer that floated on air were just a few of the glimpses into the future of 1985. For the first time, youngsters were able to drive their own car or command a boat that traveled around Tomorrowland. Within a few years, Disneyland would boast that they had one of the biggest submarine fleets in the world and the first daily running monorail system.

Boys and girls walked through the gate of Frontierland and felt what it would be like to become their favorite western heroes Davy Crocket, Zorro or the Lone Ranger. Guests could board the Mark Twain Riverboat or raft across the Rivers of America to Tom Sawyer Island to explore and even fish off the dock. Native Americans would perform daily donning authentic costumes and demonstrating the music and dance that was passed down to each generation. Guests could ride atop a donkey or ride in covered wagons through the desert to feel the struggles of the first settlers to this country.

Families could travel down a jungle river and come face to face with the wild animals they saw on the movie screens on *Disney's True-Life Adventures*. Imaginations soared as they were entertained by the birds and flowers at the Enchanted Tiki Room, seeing the new technology of animatronics with their own eyes.

With the new millennium came a brand-new theme park, Disney California Adventure, bringing the wonders of California to one place where families could see the entire state in one day.

Walking down Hollywood Boulevard brought the glamour of Hollywood right to the people. Stepping into your own limousine to visit with your favorite stars and watching the famous Muppets perform for you in 3D gave each visitor a thrill. Today, you can ride through Monstropolis to save Boo from Randall, save the Guardians of the Galaxy or watch Broadway caliber shows

Travel the forests of California around Grizzly Peak as you explore the redwood forest and watch children climb, slide and explore the world around them. Travel down the rivers of California on the roaring rapids or fly high above the wonders of California to arrive back at Disneyland just in time for an amazing fireworks display. Today guests can see the entire world is one trip that will make anyone an adventurer.

Guests could visit the Santa Monica pier and ride some vintage attractions found by this seaside retreat before finding their way to the vineyards of Northern California for a glass of wine or the pier to snack on authentic foods from the San Francisco area.

With the passing years came many changes to Disney California Adventure. New generations would experience all new areas and rides.

One of the newest areas of Disney California Adventure let's guests visit with their friends from Radiator Springs as your favorite Pixar film comes to life. Have a wild time with Mater as you square dance on your own tractor. Get your new tires at Luigi's before getting your dance move on once again. Finally, zip around the canyons as you practice for the big race at Radiator Springs Racers. When you get tired, stop at the Cozy Cone Motel for a cold drink or something to eat.

Continue your visit with your friends from Pixar as you ride the Incredicoaster and find baby Jack Jack. Hop on

*One hundred things you need to do at Disneyland before you die*

your own desert critter and ride Jessie's Critter Carousel before putting on your 3D glasses to play the games of Toy Story Mania. Visit with these larger than life characters before stopping at Bing Bongs for a sweet treat, then ride your feelings with Inside Out Emotional Whirlwind or soar above the lake on the Pixar Pal-A-Round.

While park has changed with time and a new park has grown right beside Disneyland, one thing remains steadfast, the dream of Walt Disney lives on with each guest that passes through the gates of this magical place.

If this is your first time experiencing everything that Disneyland has to offer, this book may help you decide what speaks to your heart. If this is your five-hundredth time visiting the resort, you may find something new to bring back some of the feelings you experienced the first time you came to this happy place.

Whether it is meeting Mickey Mouse or riding Space Mountain, there are hundreds of ways to make a visit to Disneyland special. Flying over London with Peter Pan, Traveling the ice-covered peak of Matterhorn, soaring over the wonders of the world or visiting Toontown with Roger Rabbit, you won't want to miss one moment.

While it is impossible to do everything at Disneyland in one visit, you can ensure you won't miss any of the magic when you have One Hundred Thing to do at Disneyland Before You Die as your companion on your visit.

# Before you enter Disneyland

With all the excitement of a trip to Disneyland, it is hard to believe you would have a list outside the theme parks but there are several things you will want to experience throughout the resort.

While guests first thoughts of the Disneyland resort are the wonders that lay beyond the front gates of the theme parks, Disney has included many wonders throughout the resort.

☐ Ride the tram from the parking areas

> From the beginnings of Disneyland resort, guests have been riding the trams provided to help bring you from your car to the front gates and back again. Originally, the park lot at Disneyland was a vast expanse of parking spaces that would fill up very quickly each day.

The parking areas were numbered and broken down into sections with character names providing a reminder of where to find your car once your day at the park was done. For those who knew the parking lot, the spaces in the Bambi or Cinderella areas were coveted. Naturally, the parking has grown as Disneyland has grown, but the tram has remained a constant to help the guests arrive at their destination in comfort.

☐ Ride the Mickey Van for handicap priority

While the majority of Disneyland guests jump aboard the many trams circling the acreage between the parking areas and the front entrance of the Disneyland resort, the Mickey van is a much lesser known option. This smaller vehicle allows those with special needs to ride with comfort and accommodate their various equipment in a smaller enclosed space.

☐ Enter Disneyland Park via the Monorail

The monorail is the wonder of the modern age. Gliding along the rail, high above the entrance to Disneyland, you get a bird eye view of the entire esplanade area.

Gaze out at the different lands, seeing Tomorrowland, Fantasyland and the hub of Disneyland before you come to the Tomorrowland station, right in the center of the excitement.

The monorail offers air-conditioned comfort from Downtown Disney for those looking for another way to travel through huge resort. For guests looking for a quick trip to Downtown Disney from Disneyland park, hop aboard at the Tomorrowland Station and let the monorail whisk you to the shopping and dining area.

☐ Find the compass at the center of the esplanade

The esplanade is the area between Disneyland and Disney California Adventure. Over the years, this area has played host to millions of happy guests arriving for a fun filled day at Disneyland. The esplanade has been a showcase for celebrities and movie openings, along with the props that bring the guests right to the magic of movie making.

Directly in the center of this area, you will find an enormous compass to help visitors along their travels. While the area outside of the theme parks has changed over the years, this area has been host to many Disneyland contests, events and celebrations of the theme park milestones.

☐ Visit the World of Disney store

Anywhere throughout the Disneyland resort you will find gift shops that will make it very difficult to pick just the right item to take home with you. Sometimes it feels impossible to find the exact item as a reminder of your amazing visit to Disneyland. But, walk through the doors of World of Disney and you have everything your heart desires before your eyes.

Whether you are looking for clothing, mouse ears, toys, books, jewelry or home goods, World of Disney can lay the choices at your feet.

This gigantic store is constantly updated with the latest styles and items that every Disney enthusiast is looking for to add to their collection.

☐ Spend time at Downtown Disney

The Downtown Disney District offer the best of Anaheim with world class shops, restaurants and entertainment.

Here you will find every kind of cuisine from all American to Creole, Mexican to Italian. Whatever you crave, you will find it here.

If bowling is your thing, stop at the themed bowling alley. For fans of Lego, pop into the Lego Store to get the latest building kit to take home. Outside the Lego Store are amazing sculptures to get great pictures with.

Stop and listen to singers, musicians and bands playing every night of the week for your enjoyment.

Stop during Mardi Gras and hear traditional jazz. Visit during the holidays to ice skate and drink hot coco.

Whatever time of year, there is always lots going on at Downtown Disney.

☐ Visit Goofy's Kitchen at the Disneyland Hotel

Spend the morning with your favorite Disney characters at Goofy's Kitchen. Indulge your tastes at the sweeping buffet in this fun atmosphere for families before heading into the theme parks.

During your meal, Mickey, Minnie, Donald, Goofy, Daisy and Pluto come right to your table for visits and for photo opportunities. Make your reservation today for Goofy's Kitchen.

☐ Visit Trader Sam's for a cool drink with an Adventureland influence

Trader Sam's at the Disneyland Hotel offers guests adult refreshment while basking in the south sea ambience of Adventureland. Notice the influence of the Enchanted Tiki Room in the idols and totems with their moving eyes. Birds and flowers complete the picture along with various items from your favorite Adventureland attractions.

During the holidays, Trader Sam's has offered Haunted Mansion inspired tiki mugs as well as holiday inspired cocktails.

There is something refreshing waiting for you in the jungle at Trader Sam's.

☐ Book a room at the Grand Californian Hotel and get early admission to Disney California Adventure

The Grand Californian Hotel is a marvel of the Disneyland resort. Designed in the arts and crafts era of California, the hotel is exquisite in every detail. As you enter the enormous lobby, you will be amazed at the open beam ceilings, stained glass windows and stone fireplace that keeps guests warm on cool evenings. Enjoy a live pianist as they entertain guests with a variety of Disney tunes.

While the hotel and rooms are incredibly comfortable, one perk of staying at the Grand Californian is the secret entrance into Disney California Adventure park for guests of the hotel.

Wake up early and get your day started at Disney California Adventure before any other resort guests.

☐ Stay at the Disneyland Hotel

The Disneyland hotel goes hand in hand with Disneyland as a classic of the Disney empire. In

1955, just months before the opening of Disneyland, ground broke on the hotel just across the road from the new theme park.

The hotel opened in October 1955, with only a handful of rooms available for reservations. It would be in August 1956, that the hotel would be complete with three-hundred rooms available for guests to book.

Today, there are close to one thousand rooms available from standard rooms to luxury suites to themed suites, there is something for every taste at the Disneyland resort.

☐ Stay at Paradise Pier hotel

This beach themed hotel is another jewel in the crown of the Disneyland resort. Stay just across from the bustling Downtown Disney District with sparkling outdoor pools.

Be sure to rise early to get your extra magic hours at Disneyland and Disney California Adventure.

☐ Say "I Do" at Disneyland resort

For the engaged couples looking for the perfect fairy tale wedding, Disneyland resort offers wedding packages for every budget. From those wanting an intimate ceremony or the ultimate extravaganza, look to the wedding specialists to create your dream come true.

Every bride will feel like a princess and every groom will be Prince Charming at this once in a lifetime event.

☐ Join the Disney Vacation Club

For those wanting more vacation for the money, the Disney Vacation Club offers a wide variety of vacation options for every budget. For your monthly fee, guests can stay on Disney property at theme parks resorts worldwide. Take a Disney cruise to immerse your family in Disney magic on the high seas. Disney offers guest vacations tailored to each guest tastes, so explore the world with the Disney Vacation Club.

# Disneyland

The history of Disneyland resort begins with the first theme park of this spectacular dynasty. Disneyland opened July 17, 1955 with a chaotic opening. Fifteen thousand tickets had been sold, but twenty-eight thousand people showed up with some tickets being forged and sold to unsuspecting guests. This new theme park was unable to handle to additional people entering the gates, and soon, food and beverages had run out.

With the frantic pace for the builders, many of the attractions were not fully operational, and the guests experienced ride malfunctions throughout the day. Adding to the difficulties that Disneyland experienced were extreme heat that caused the new asphalt to melt as people walked down Main Street U.S.A.

Walt Disney gave a brief opening day speech so the happy guests could explore the new park rather than listen to him drone on. Future president Ronald Reagan attended the opening as a member of the press giving real time reports from Disneyland in the televised opening day. Walt Disney's long-time friend Art Linkletter officially emceed the event, giving guests a preview of the wonders they would encounter when they arrived at this happy place.

Despite the opening day problems, Disneyland thrived and expanded to include new themed areas like Critter Country and Toontown. With these new areas came new attractions to delight and thrill millions of guests each year.

Disneyland has celebrated milestones through the years and included each guest that walks through the gates. The twentieth anniversary in 1975, thirty-fifth in 1990, the fiftieth in 2005 and the sixtieth in 2015 brought the legacy of Disneyland resort to the guests which made the theme park a success.

Now, you have the opportunity to see every aspect of Disneyland with this book. If you find one new detail to add to your Disneyland excitement, then I have succeeded in my quest to bring guests something new.

# Main Street

The history of Main Street U.S.A. began with Walt Disney as a young boy when his family moved from Chicago Illinois to Marceline, Missouri when Walt was just four years old. Walt Disney talked about his time in Marceline as his favorite time of his life and revisited the family farm in 1956 with his wife Lillian.

When Walt Disney began plans for Disneyland, he wanted his guests to experience the small town he grew up in and thus, Main Street U.S.A. was born. While the street has changed over the years with shop fronts changing and new faces replacing the old cast, Main Street has never changed for one reason, it will always remain a thank you from Walt to his beloved Marceline.

☐ Be choose as the family of the day

> Each day before the gate of Disneyland open, hundreds of people stand waiting for their day at this happy place to begin. While it would be enough

just to open the gates, and let the guests explore the magic, Disneyland always does things in just the right way to bring a little extra excitement to the beginning of the day.

One family is selected from the crowd and invited to the large area just inside the gates. The cast members announce this family and they lead the crowd in the countdown to open Disneyland park.

If you are interested in a chance at this amazing experience, arrive very early and hope the cast members look your way.

☐ Stand on the platform at the Disneyland Railroad Main Street Station and get a picture of Main Street U.S.A.

Disneyland is one of the most amazing spectacles you will have the delight in seeing. While seeing the park from street level is a thrill, walking the steps to the Disneyland Railroad Main Street Station will give you a bird's eye view of the park that will bring a chill to your skin.

Just take a few moments to revel in this wonderful view of Main Street U.S.A. with Sleeping Beauty Castle framing the picture perfectly. Snap pictures from this vantage point before going on with your day at Disneyland.

☐ Explore the history of the Disneyland Railroad in the shadow boxes at the Disneyland Railroad Main Street Station

Within the train station, guests will be transported back in time to the beginnings of Disneyland. Within the shadow boxes, guests will find tickets, magazines, miniature models and a variety of other memorabilia that shows the history of this attraction since the opening day of Disneyland.

Spend a few moments looking over this great collection to get a better understanding and deeper love of Walt Disney and his lifelong love of trains.

☐ Look in the ticket office of the Disneyland Railroad Mai Street Station

Most guests entering the platform of the Disneyland Railroad Main Street Station walk right past the ticket office without ever stopping or even noticing this small area. For those that spend a few moments looking in the window, they get a glimpse to the detail that the imagineers put into Disneyland.

Within the ticket office, you will see a moment frozen in time. Look on the stool and see the gloves waiting for their owner to reappear. Manuals line the back wall, even a schedule of ticket costs posted on the wall including the cost for small children to travel cross country.

This small space was not left without amazing details which is another example of the loving attention the developers put into Disneyland.

☐ Ride the Disneyland railroad from the Main Street Station

Whether you are traveling to a specific area of Disneyland or want a complete circle tour of the theme park, the Disneyland Railroad offers a unique view of the areas of the theme park not seen in any other way.

From the moment you board the various trains, named after those closest to Walt Disney, your narrator gives details about Main Street, New Orleans Square, Fantasyland and Tomorrowland.

One of the most amazing attractions missed by most visitors to Disneyland is the diorama of the Grand Canyon complete with wildlife. Travel along the rim of the canyon, then back in time to see dinosaurs and prehistoric insects thrive then become extinct in this thrilling attraction.

☐ Get your birthday button and birthday call from Mickey Mouse at City Hall on Main Street U.S.A.

Every day, thousands of people young and old visit Disneyland on their birthday and the theme park has been waiting for you with a special button to commemorate your day. Just visit City Hall on Main Street and get your button on your way into the park. The cast members around Disneyland will be sure to offer their own Happy Birthday greeting as you spend your happy day with them.

Don't want to wait in line at City Hall? Go to any of the shops on Main Street and get the same experience. If you are one of the thousands of people celebrating their birthday at Disneyland, you definitely want to make a public announcement by wearing this special birthday button. Cast members love to make these buttons customized with your age or special messages just for you. In addition, Mickey Mouse is waiting to give you his own birthday message for visiting him on your special day.

Just because you are not the birthday boy or girl does not mean you cannot be in on the fun. Be sure to get your I'm Celebrating button to show you're with someone special. Not your birthday? Get your Happily Ever After button for your honeymoon or your Graduation button during the months of May and June.

☐ See the awards Disneyland has received inside City Hall

The City Hall building on Main Street is more than just guest services. If you look at the framed photos along the walls, you will see a timeline of Disneyland itself. Photos of Walt Disney and the many awards that show how Disneyland has grown over the years are displayed with pride in this very special building.

As you are taking your tour of City Hall, be sure to stop at the small bookshelf and peek at the titles within. You will recognize some of your favorite Disney films in the titles. Another fun nod to Disney history are the books resting on their side. Lillibelle by W.E.D. and Mickey Mouse with the famous Disney D.

☐ Take one of the famous Disneyland tours

Go deeper into the history of Disneyland by taking a tour.

Many tours have been given throughout the history of Disneyland, giving guests an inside look at the workings of Disneyland in a very personal way. The "Walk in Walt's Disneyland Footsteps" tour has been offered to guests for many years giving guests a special inside look at the development of Disneyland along with VIP boarding for certain attractions. While this tour changes throughout the year, the flavor of the tour remains constant. The tour guides trained for the "Walking in Walt's Footsteps" tours are some of the most knowledgeable guides Disney has to offer, so drink in every moment of this exclusive look at the Disneyland resort.

Periodically, guests will get additional thrills added to these tours like the opportunity to see Walt Disney's private apartment or ride in the Lillie Belle car on the train. These special touches add to the distinct memories each person takes with them at the end of their tour.

During the holiday months, look for specialty tours like Holidaytime at Disneyland or Happiest Haunts during Halloween.

☐ Ride on the Omnibus

Weary travelers on Main Street U.S.A. can hop aboard a classic omnibus, an open-air double decker bus that will take you right to Sleeping Beauty Castle.

The omnibus offers a different view above street level giving guests a fantastic picture opportunity of Main Street or Sleeping Beauty Castle.

☐ Travel down Main Street on the horse drawn streetcar

Another of the Main Street vehicles is the only non-motorized car in the livery. This antique streetcar began taking guests from the entrance of Main Street to Sleeping Beauty Castle when Disneyland opened, along with the horse drawn firetruck which is now parked at the Main Street Fire Station.

The horse drawn streetcar gives guests an opportunity to slow down and take in the sights of Main Street as the streetcar is pulled by one of the Disney Clydesdales.

Ask the attendant if you can pet the animals, most enjoy interacting with the guests but remember, they are working so please ask before approaching these magnificent horses.

Keep an eye out for the Dapper Dans, as they will board the streetcar and serenade the guests traveling aboard.

☐ Take a ride on the Disneyland Firetruck

This replica of a 1916 firetruck was added to the Main Street vehicles in 1958. Walt Disney wanted guest to experience a real working town on Main Street U.S.A. which included working vehicles along the roadways.

Climb aboard and ring the bell as you take a trip down Main Street U.S.A. Be sure to get an honorary fire badge sticker for your little firemen from the driver before you exit the vehicle to continue your magical day.

*One hundred things you need to do at Disneyland before you die*

☐  Stop to listen to the Dapper Dan's sing for you

While Disneyland is widely known for the rides and fireworks, the entertainment cannot be compared. The Dapper Dan's have been a mainstay of Main Street U.S.A. practically since the park opening. Not only do the Dapper Dan's voices blend perfectly but these talents young men also tap dance and play the organ chimes.

While you can listen to the Dapper Dan's performing daily, you may find them in various places throughout the entrance to Disneyland. Sometimes you may get a serenade on the street car or may even find them singing on their bicycle built for four. No matter where you find them, it is worth time spent with The Dapper Dan's.

☐  Listen to the Main Street musicians entertain you

Main Street U.S.A. is always abuzz with various sights, smells and sounds but the sweetest sound you will hear are the various musicians that entertain guests on their way into the happiest place on earth.

The Straw Hatters play their Dixieland and turn of the century tunes for guests. Look for the Main Street piano player with his ragtime Disneyland tunes at Coca Cola™ corner as you rest from your travels through Main Street U.S.A.

☐ Visit Walt Disney's apartment above the fire station on Main Street U.S.A.

Even though you cannot access the apartment itself, you can stand below and see the ever-present lamp that burns in memory of Disneyland's founder.

During the construction of Disneyland, Walt Disney had this apartment built so he could stay overnight on the property and give Disneyland his undivided attention. Walt and his wife, Lillian, made this a home for themselves and their children and grandchildren during their time at Disneyland. The Disney legends that helped Walt realize his dream, have told stories of Walt rising early in the morning to walk down Main Street and survey the work done the day before.

After Disneyland's opening, Walt loved to visit the Sunkist shop and play with the machine that squeezed the oranges into juice. For Christmas, the cast bought Walt his very own juicer, that still resides in the apartment unused, since Walt's joy was in playing with the large machine on Main Street.

☐ Stop for a visit at the Main Street fire station

This fire station houses a genuine horse drawn fire truck. Be sure to climb up on the seat and pose for a picture on this piece of history. Notice the horse stalls with the names of the horses still waiting for them to return from a fire.

Notice the fire pole within the fire station. Walt Disney himself slid down this pole when in residence. The access from Walt Disney's apartment has long since been closed over to ensure guests do not try to climb up from below. This fireman's pole is a reminder of Walt's attention to detail and his ever-present childlike wonder of the world.

☐ Read Walt Disney's opening day speech at the base of the flagpole

On opening day, July 17, 1955, Walt Disney read a short but poignant speech welcoming guests to Disneyland. To commemorate this event, a small bronze plaque with his words was erected at the base of the flagpole on Main Street U.S.A. Make a pilgrimage to this area to give thanks to the vision of this great man and read his words.

☐ Watch the flag retreat ceremony

Walt Disney was a true American, joining the Armed Forced as a teenager to do his duty to the country that gave him so much. When making Disneyland a reality, Disney included the flagpole at the center of Main Street to fly the American Flag high above this amazing theme park.

Each day, guests gather here to watch the cast members create a solemn time to retire the flag with the Disneyland band and the Dapper Dans playing the music that celebrates our country. Cast members who have honored the country with their service bring the flag down and fold it while guests who have served stand in places of honor around the flagpole.

Do not miss this amazing event each afternoon at Disneyland park.

☐ Get pictures with your favorite Disney characters on Main Street U.S.A.

Each day, thousands of guests enter Disneyland and walk through the entrance to be greeted by their favorite classic Disney characters. Mickey Mouse, Minnie Mouse, Donald Duck, Daisy Duck, Goofy and Pluto pose for pictures and sign autograph for the young and young at heart.

Do not miss your chance to get pictures with these icons of Disney cartoons.

☐ Visit the Disneyana shop to see one of a kind and limited-edition artwork from Disney artists

Within Disneyana you will find not only authentic Disneyland souvenirs, but one of a kind works of art from artists all over the world. You will also find

Disney artists showing off their expertise in drawing classic characters daily within this shop. Be sure to order your own sketch of your favorite character for your collection.

Notice the vault within this shop. This is the last remnant of the bank that was housed in this building when Disneyland first opened in 1955. When Disneyland opened, Bank of America™ was opened daily to allow guests to do their banking and get cash during their visit. The teller windows cut the main room in half to allow the bankers to do their work.

If you visit the second and third rooms, this was not always a part of this store. This area actually housed the replica of Walt Disney's office, complete with his actual desk and trinkets on display for guests to see until this artifact was moved to Walt Disney World to be a part of the Walt, One Man's Dream attraction, a walk-through museum of the life of Walt Disney.

Not only does this shop hold fantastic works of art, several times a year authors come to sign their latest book within this shop.

*Catherine F. Olen*

☐ Visit the Main Street Opera House to see the bench, carousel horse and peanut cart commemorating the place where Walt Disney first envisioned Disneyland

The artifacts at the entrance to the Main Street Opera House are actually brought to Disneyland from Griffith Park in Los Angeles. It was in this park that Walt Disney first had the inspiration that would become Disneyland. The story, as told by Walt Disney, talks about Sunday being daddy daughter day and he would take his girls to Griffith Park in Los Angeles to ride the carousel. While he enjoyed watching his girls play on the antique carousel, he would sit on the bench and eat peanuts passively sine there were no attractions in the park for the three of them to enjoy together.

It was here that Disney imagined a place where parents and children could interact together, bring their family closer during their visit. Thus, the dream of Disneyland was born on this very bench.

☐ Find a large map encased behind glass within the Main Street Opera House.

This map is the original design for Disneyland resort.

This large map shows the attractions that opened at Disneyland on July 17, 1955. A far cry from the Disneyland we know today, this map gives guests a glimpse into Walt Disney's original vision of the theme park.

If you examine this map, you will see the attraction around the park that have long since retired like the Chicken of the Sea pirates ship and the Motor Boat Cruise. Several of the attractions on this map still exist in the Disneyland we know today like the Jungle Cruise and the Mark Twain Riverboat.

Spend some time admiring the origins of Disneyland before enjoying the attractions that exist today.

☐ Find the Disneyland newspaper within the Opera House

Mounted on the wall near the large map of Disneyland, you will find a replica of the newspaper printed to share the events of opening day.

This reproduction of the Disneyland newspaper allows guests to read all about that famous day, July 17, 1955. Find out how many people joined in on the fun, which attractions were running or a variety of little details that will make you feel like you were right there.

☐ See props and costumes from your favorite new Disney films

The Walt Disney Studios is thrilling audiences with new films each year and the Main Street Opera House brings guests close to the action with costumes worn by your favorite actors and props used in these dazzling films.

These original live action movies reinvent the classic animated films for a new generation. This constantly changing museum offers a glimpse into the world of film making.

Many new films that have been featured in this area include *Mary Poppins Returns*, *Dumbo* and *Aladdin*. Keep an eye out for the next film in this ever-changing display.

☐ In the waiting area for Great Moments with Mr. Lincoln you will find a scale model of The Capitol Building in Washington D.C.

Take some time to look at the original artwork and statuary lining the walls of this room.

This model of the Capitol building was built in 1935 by artist George H. Lloyd, and sold to Walt Disney by the artist in 1955 at the urging of Disney to include it in what he named liberty square at the time. The artist agreed to terms and this replica has been house here at the Main Street Opera House to amazed guests ever since.

☐ Find the childhood photo of Walt Disney inside the Main Street Opera House

Hidden within the Main Street Opera House is a wonderful photograph of Walt Disney and his good friend, Walt Pfeiffer, dressed for a school play.

This small photo shows a glimpse of the showman Walt Disney would become while seeing the enchanting young man enjoying his life in his small town. The photo is well hidden so simply ask a cast member or hunt through the room till you find this treasure of Disney's origins.

☐ Spend some time with President Lincoln as you hear his immortal words once more in one of Walt Disney's favorite attractions, Great Moments with Mr. Lincoln

Walt Disney openly admired President Abraham Lincoln and decided early in the design of Disneyland to include the president in his theme park. While the reality would not take place until 1964, Walt worked with his imagineers to push the boundaries of audio animatronics to create President Lincoln. The face of the president was sculpted using photographs and a life cast of Lincolns head. The show you are about to see premiered at the World's Fair in 1964.

The press would stretch the truth about the exhibit by claiming that President Lincoln actually walked off the stage and shook hands with guests of the attraction. While this was never the case, Great Moments with Mr. Lincoln will make you proud to be in his presence for a brief moment.

☐ Be sure to pick up the most well-known souvenir at Disneyland resort, Mouse ears.

The famous Mickey Mouse Ears have grown to offer a variety of style to suit ever guest.

Throughout the history of Disneyland, one icon has been head and ears above the rest.

The iconic Mickey Mouse ears debuted on The Mickey Mouse c=Club in 1955 with children all over the United States wanting a pair of the ears for their very own. While you can no longer get your name hand embroidered on the ears, technology has taken over to offer a variety of fonts and colors for your name.

Disneyland has expanded throughout the years to include hundreds of different mouse ears and headbands including almost every character and attraction in the Disney family, as well as holiday ears and custom designs.

☐ See the animated window displays at Emporium

As you walk along the sidewalk in front of the Emporium shop on Main Street, you will notice several windows with scenes from your favorite animated Disney films adorning the windows. Watch as the scenes magically change to reveal the characters in classic scenes, while lighting effects make these window displays come to life right before your eyes.

☐ Visit the Main Street Magic Shop for a free demonstration

Main Street Magic has been a permanent fixture on Main Street U.S.A. for decades but few guests who visit Disneyland know that just inside are some of the most talented cast members at Disneyland resort. The artists in this shop will be happy to demonstrate the illusions available for purchase and love to interact with the kids who wander into this shop.

Enjoy the talent of the magicians or book an early morning class for guests staying in Disney hotels.

Be sure to find the autograph picture of actor, comedian and former Main Street Magic employee Steve Martin hanging on the wall behind the counter.

☐ Lift the receiver of the phone in Main Street Magic and listen to a turn of the century party line

> Back in the origins of the telephone, each person did not have their own phone line. You could pick up your phone to hear others having a conversation any time of the day. These phones found here and in Starbucks demonstrate what it was like to live during the first years of the telephone.
>
> Enjoy listening in on the conversation but be careful or you might get caught by the parties as you listen in on their secrets.

☐ Visit the Emporium and see the turn of the century scenes above the main floor

> Thousands of guests enter the Emporium shop each day to find just the right souvenir to take home with them from Disneyland. Very few take the time to look just above their heads at the detailed scenes depicting every day life in the turn of the century.
>
> Enjoy the antics of a small boy getting his hair cut or admire the lovely hats on display in the millenary shop.
>
> The attention to detail at Disneyland never ends as each guest gets a new experience each time they enter this beloved shop.

☐ See the classic characters in the scenes above toy department at Emporium

In the toy section of Emporium is a charming area that delights guests each day. Your favorite Disney characters are waiting to greet you as they play in this adorable setting. Find Robin Hood and Marion on the teeter totter, Captain Hook by the large windows and Buzz Lightyear getting ready for his next mission. Do not miss this very sweet area of Emporium next time you are on Main Street.

☐ Visit the Main Street Cinema to watch some of the earliest Mickey Mouse cartoon shorts

Housed in this small cinema, you will find treasure beyond belief while you watch the original cartoons by animation visionary Walt Disney. Here you will find *Steamboat Willie*, *Plane Crazy*, *Mickey's Polo Team*, *The Dog Napper* and *The Moose Hunt* playing from the moment Disneyland opens. Hidden among these classic cartoons is the only time Pluto speaks on film, so do not miss this hidden gem.

Be sure to buy your ticket from Tilly who has manned the ticket booth since Disneyland opened. If you visit Disneyland throughout the year, you will notice Tilly's dress and the décor within the ticket book change to match the seasons.

☐ Get your picture in front of the Disneyland Casting Agency door next to the Main Street Cinema

This tribute to founder Walt Disney is a must see on your travels down Main Street U.S.A.

If you stop to look around Main Street U.S.A. you will notice the windows on the second story pay homage to the animators and imagineers that made Disney's visions a reality. The door you see before you, is the perfect love letter to Walt Disney as the quote you see below his name was Disney's reality. Disney understood that he could never achieve his goals alone and created the best possible team around him in whatever endeavor he had his hand in currently.

Make sure to get your picture in front of this door on your way down Main Street U.S.A.

☐ Listen to the dentist drilling a bad tooth at E.S. Blitz Painless Dentist in the small cross street near the locker area on Main Street U.S.A.

Disney was the master of details. E.S. Blitz dentistry in this little corner of Main Street is an excellent example. Not only do you see what it was like during the turn of the century, but you can hear it all around you.

The dentist office door can be found in the hidden alcove near the lockers but the dentist office can be found on the second floor. If you stand below and listen, you can hear one unfortunate patient having a tooth drilled.

☐ Listen to piano lessons on the second floor over Clothiers

Take a few moments to listen to the piano teacher in town give a lesson to one of her prize pupils. You might hear some wrong notes if you stay too long.

The sights and sounds of turn of the century living can be found in every corner of Main Street.

☐ Listen to the private investigator in his office on Main Street U.S.A.

From time to time, you will hear the famous private investigator on his phone or hear his dog barking while he waits for his next big case.

☐ Find the wall that built Disneyland

At the end of the small cross street that leads to the lockers on Main Street, you will find what appears to be a plain brick wall to the right of the doorway for the locker area. If you look very closely, you will notice that this small wall has three different types of brick.

During the construction of Disneyland, this wall was put into place so Walt Disney could point to the type of brick he wanted in any area of the park at a glance. Instead of destroying this sample wall, the cast kept it to pay homage to Walt Disney.

☐ Eat on the patio at Carnation Café

Spend some time on the patio at the Carnation Café while enjoying this open-air dining experience on Main Street while eating classic American fare.

Carnation Café was one of the original businesses on Main Street opening day in 1955 serving ice cream to guests. The area that now houses the patio seating was actually an outdoor flower market on opening day, where guests could purchase faux flowers as souvenirs.

It was not until 1997 that the ice cream parlor closed and Disneyland created this lovely dining experience.

☐ Taste handmade ice cream at the Gibson Girl Ice Cream Shop

For a cool treat on a hot day, stop in the Gibson Girls Ice Cream Shop for your favorite flavors. Originally opening in 1997, Gibson Girl has offered guests these tasty treats for decades.

A fun piece of trivia, Disneyland has sold enough ice cream to fill the Matterhorn mountain.

☐ Watch the candy makers at Candy Palace make hand make sweets for guests to take home

These talented artisans create handmade candy sold daily within this shop.

Candy Palace is a must do during your time at Disneyland. Sweets of every variety are contained within the walls of Candy Palace, but this shop has something you will not find anywhere else in the park.

Candy artisans are busy at work daily creating classic sweets to be sold that day. Peanut brittle, rocky road and chocolate cover toffee are just a sample of the delights created in this window.

During the holidays, the candy artists create handmade candy canes and guests arrive hours before park opening to get a wrist band so they can take home these delectable peppermint canes before the holiday season is over.

- ☐ Watch some silent films in the penny flicker machines in at the Penny Arcade

    At the front of Penny Arcade, you will find antique flickers, the predecessor to the modern movies starring the biggest stars of their day.

    Drop your penny in the slot to watch Charlie Chaplin or Laurel and Hardy perform for you. These charming flickers are a must see during your time in Penny Arcade.

- ☐ Be sure to test yourself on the electricity machine, the kissing machine or get your fortune told with Esmeralda

    Go back to the turn of century and see what it was like in a real Penny Arcade. Within Penny Arcade you will find yet another celebrity at Disneyland. Esmeralda will tell your fortune for just a small fee. Be sure to pick up your fortune card when Esmeralda is through reading your cards.

    For the braver guests, literally try your hand at the electricity machine and see if you can endure.

    At the rear of Penny Arcade, you will find the kissing machine to see how great a lover you are. But it is the item next to the kissing machine that is the hidden gem. The nickelodeon will play for you every seven minutes and is a wonder of the machine age. Playing multiple instruments at the same time, this antique will play a variety of classic Disney songs for your pleasure.

☐ Let Pinocchio dance for you for a small fee

The little marionette stands waiting for guests to feed a coin into the slot and make him come to life as he dances to the strains of your favorite Disney songs. This little wooden puppet loves to make guest happy during their time in the Penny Arcade.

☐ Sit on the porch on Main Street U.S.A.

As you walk down Main Street you will see shops lining this pleasant street. You probably do not expect to see guests resting on the porch of one of these shops but you will see just that.

In the early days of Disneyland, this building house the Wizard of Bras, a short-lived lingerie shop. Now it stands next door to The China Closet store and allows guests a fantastic view of the parades or a rest for their tired feet.

☐ Get your silhouette done on Main Street

In a small shop on Main Street stands a workshop that has been creating one of a kind souvenirs since the park opened in 1955. These artists create seamless cuts to capture the likeness of guests offering a very reasonably priced souvenir.

When you visit the silhouette shop, look around and you may recognize the likenesses of Mark Twain, Sherlock Holmes, Abraham Lincoln and you may see a very famous mouse in the group silhouettes.

☐ Visit Coca Cola corner

This small shop has the most dazzling array of stained glass at Disneyland. The stained glass and variety of antique bottles in the window advertise the soft drink sold within.

Also find the red and white light bulb, one of the best kept secrets within the theme park. If you look beneath the awning at the corner of the building, you will see red and white lights chasing around the small space. In order to keep the bulbs even and thus avoiding two red or two white bulbs together, the imagineers created this red and white bulb which, if you look very closely, does not actually light.

☐ Stop and listen to the piano player at Coca Cola™ Corner

As you spend time at Coca Cola™ Corner in the outdoor patio, you will find a white upright piano. Here you will be entertained by some of the best ragtime piano players you will have the fortune to hear.

It is not a coincidence that you recognize several classic Disney songs from your favorite films, but you will also hear classics from the turn of the century like *The Maple Leaf Rag* by Scott Joplin.

☐ Visit the Jolly Holiday Bakery

Looking for an early morning treat or dessert during your time at Disneyland?

Jolly Holiday Bakery has everything to tempt you. While famous for their sweets, they also offer a full array of sandwiches if you are looking for something heartier.

While you are visiting Jolly Holiday, be sure to notice the stained-glass penguins, the lyrics from your favorite songs and nick knacks in the curios. All of these little touches are a love poem to the film *Mary Poppins* which was the inspiration for the name of the bakery as well as the décor.

☐ Visit Photo shop for all your camera needs

While the Photo Shop on Main Street may seem like a self-explanatory shop, this shop holds more than just your camera needs.

Check out your PhotoPass pictures with experts assisting you in choosing the package that works for your budget. Pick up SD cards and extra batteries for your devices. But a little-known fact of Photo Shop is the battery drop off where these cast members will take your battery and charge it for you while you are exploring the Magic Kingdom. Just stop off and pick up your fully charge battery for your camera or video recording device when you need it.

☐ See Walt Disney's baby picture within the baby center

The baby center offers families a quiet, private place to take care of infant needs during your stay at Disneyland. Another of the best kept secrets of Disneyland includes the baby picture of Walt Disney just inside the door of this private area.

Feel free to step inside the door to glance at Walt Disney or get a quick picture of this icon.

☐ Visit First Aid for all your medical needs

While we hope no one needs the first aid facility at Disneyland during their stay, the cast members working this area are the best in their field. Whether you need a bandage, pain killers or more advance medical assistance, just step inside this quiet area and ask the registered nurses working to help you.

These trained professionals also assist with more urgent, critical medical problems, bringing guests help where ever you may be throughout the resort.

*One hundred things you need to do at Disneyland before you die*

☐ Get a corn dog from the Little Red Wagon

> For those looking for a hearty treat to grab while they go on to the next attraction, stop at the Little Red Wagon for a hand dripped corn dog. Complete with chips and a drink, these corn dogs will keep you going throughout your day at Disneyland.

☐ Enjoy breakfast with your favorite Disney characters at Plaza Inn

> Each day on the patio of Plaza Inn, guests have an amazing breakfast but the food is not the only one reason that guests make reservations for this area of the park.
>
> During your meal, favorite Disney characters join in the fun to greet guests, sign autographs and pose for pictures. While others can look on from the sidewalk, only those invited to the party can be included in the fun at Plaza Inn.

☐ Enjoy a sumptuous meal at Plaza Inn

> Plaza Inn offers a wide variety of comfort food throughout the day for hungry guests looking for a delicious meal.
>
> Whether you are looking for fried chicken or pot roast or a salad, Plaza Inn has something for everyone.

The building the houses the Plaza Inn was purchased by Walt Disney and moved to the park with decorative wood trim and elaborate décor throughout. Be sure to explore this amazing building during your meal as it is a feast for the eyes.

- [ ] Use the utility walkway to bypass the crowds of Main Street during parades

    Normally, this walkway access is closed to the public but, during parades, the doors near Showcase shop are opened to allow the guests a clear path through to Tomorrowland.

    Keep an eye out for these open doors during your stay at Disneyland.

# Hub

The Hub of Disneyland is the central location where guests can access many of the different lands. Whether you are looking for adventures in Tomorrowland or finding your favorite stories come to life in Fantasyland, you will come through the Hub of Disneyland.

☐ Stop in the hub to take a picture with the famous Partners statue of Disneyland creator Walt Disney and his creation, Mickey Mouse

　　While Walt Disney never wanted Disneyland to be about himself, the cast who worked on Disneyland felt it would enhance the park to include this amazing statue.

　　Dedicated on November 18, 1993, Walt Disney is holding the hand of his most famous creation, Mickey Mouse. The sculptor depicted Disney in 1960 but the statue stands 6'5" while Disney only stood 5'10".

At all times of day, you will find guests standing in line to be the next one to have their picture taken with this iconic statue with Sleeping Beauty Castle towering in the background.

- [ ] Visit with your favorite Disney characters in bronze around the hub of Disneyland

    Silently looking on at guests taking their picture with Walt and Mickey are the characters that made Disney cartoons and films famous. Goofy, Chip and Dale, Minnie Mouse, Donald Duck and Dumbo are just a few of the characters waiting for you to take pictures with them before you commence your travels through Disneyland.

- [ ] Stop to smell the flowers around the hub of Disneyland

    The floral décor throughout Disneyland resort is beyond compare, but the hub of Disneyland is a wonder for the eyes. The flowers throughout this area are changed with the passing seasons as well as designed for the Halloween and Christmas holidays. The hanging baskets are painstakingly designed by the Disneyland floral department and the planters maintained to perfection before each opening day.

    Wonder at the talented artistry of the Disneyland garden department on your way through the hub of Disneyland.

# Fantasyland

The crown jewel in Disneyland resort, Fantasyland, allows guests to relive the fairy tales you grew up watching on the movie screen. With Sleeping Beauty Castle towering high above the entirety of Disneyland, just beyond her gates you will find the stories come to life as you ride along with Peter Pan, Pinocchio, Snow White and Dumbo in this most enchanting of lands.

☐ Walk up the drawbridge through Sleeping Beauty Castle

This icon of Disneyland has a working drawbridge, although it has only been used twice since the opening of Disneyland. On opening day, the children were invited to run across the drawbridge into Fantasyland for the first glimpse of this new land.

In the 1980's, Fantasyland went through a major reconstruction and the drawbridge was once again lowered for guests to experience the new and improved Fantasyland.

☐ Visit the Disneyland Time Castle

In front of Sleeping Beauty castle, you will find a non-descript plaque dedicating the Disneyland Time Castle. This time capsule was place on the 40$^{th}$ anniversary of Disneyland to be opened on July 17, 2035 on the 80$^{th}$ anniversary of Disneyland.

Some of the items included are: An "Inside Disneyland Today" Brochure for July 17, A Disneyland Cast Member Name Tag with the name "Mickey", Indiana Jones Adventure Opening Day Memorabilia, 1995 Disney Dollars and Signature Scroll—Thought on the Past, Present and Future of Disneyland, with signatures from Michael D. Eisner, Roy E. Disney, Judson C. Green, Marty Sklar, John Hench, Richard Nunis, Paul Pressler, Ray Van De Warker, Bob Penfield.

☐ Join the Disneyland Band in front of Sleeping Beauty Castle

Throughout the day in front of Sleeping Beauty Castle, the Disneyland Band performs songs from your favorite Disney films. Joined by Mickey, Minnie, Donald, Goofy and Pluto, they lead the audience in singing along with this all-star performing group.

Be sure to stop by to tap your toes and clap your hands along with the music of these talented musicians.

☐ Find the Disney family crest on Sleeping Beauty Castle

Among the beautiful decoration adorning Sleeping Beauty Castle stands a small plaque with three lions across a shield. This Disney family crest stands above the entrance to Fantasyland as a testament to the memory of Walt Disney.

☐ Make a wish at the wishing well

To the right of Sleeping Beauty Castle is Snow White grotto where you can make your wishes come true and listen to Snow White serenade you. The marble statue of Snow White and the seven dwarves stand silently greeting guests who have a wish to make.

While this charming area draws guests with the waterfall and statuary, there is a little-known fact about the characters you see before you. If you look closely at the statue of Snow White, she is the same size as the dwarf's statues. This was a mistake on the part of the artist as he was supposed to make the Snow White much larger than the rest.

To fix the mistake, the imagineers put Snow White up at the top of the water fall and the force perspective makes her appear larger than the dwarves.

Listen as Snow White will sing her song about finding true love in this charming setting.

☐ Get pictures with your favorite characters at the wishing well

Throughout the day, many of your favorite Disney characters will appear at the wishing well to pose for pictures and sign autographs for guests visiting the kingdom. You may even see the Fairy Godmother from Cinderella or the Evil Queen from Snow White ready to sign your book and pose with their fans.

☐ Stop off at the Fantasy Faire Royal theater to hear your favorite stories told

This small open-air theater allows guest to watch their favorite stories come to life. From *Beauty and the Beast* to *Tangled*, smaller guests can sit right at the front to interact with their favorite characters.

Mr. Smythe and Mr. Jones are your hosts for the retelling of these stories and, sometimes even like to put their own spin on the stories. But in the end, they all live happily ever after.

*One hundred things you need to do at Disneyland before you die*

☐ Visit the princesses at the Royal Hall

> Join the Disney princesses at Royal Hall and get your picture taken in style as you are greeted by three of your favorite princesses. Have your cameras and autograph books ready for this once in a lifetime experience created especially for you.
>
> Outside this meet and greet you can find Merida from the Pixar film *Brave*, as well as, Rapunzel and Flynn Rider from *Tangled* periodically beneath the umbrellas. Stop at Fantasy Faire to see your favorite Fairytale princess come to life.

☐ Find Rapunzel looking down from her tower at Fantasy Faire

> Sitting in the center of the courtyard of Fantasy Faire, guests will find the tower from Tangled with Rapunzel looking out her window longing to join in the fun below.
>
> Most guests walk right through this area of the theme park without ever realizing that they are being spied on from this well-known tower.

☐ Find Clopin's music box in Fantasy Faire

> Within Fantasy Faire stands a small music box Clopin from *The Hunchback of Notre Dame* stands within waiting to perform for guests visiting this

small corner of Fantasyland. Turn the handle and hear your favorite tune from this classic film.

If you look very closely within the crowd surrounding Clopin, you will find many of your favorite Disney characters throughout the throngs of people.

☐ Find the princess thrones in the walkway of Sleeping Beauty Castle

If you walk through the walkway from Fantasy Faire through the castle, you will come across a large window with several thrones within. Look very carefully and you will notice tell-tale signs of each princess in each chair. Perhaps an apple or a sea shell might give away the owner or even some mice friends might be close by to reveal the princess who owns a particular throne.

☐ Find the diorama from *Sleeping Beauty* in the castle shop

Within the shop in Sleeping Beauty Castle, you will find a diorama behind the register of Sleeping Beauty in the forest with her woodland friends. This wonderful moment from this classic Disney film has been immortalized for guest to enjoy all year long.

If you listen carefully, you can hear Aurora singing the classic *Once Upon a Dream* while fantasizing about her dream prince.

*One hundred things you need to do at Disneyland before you die*

☐ Find a bronze statue of Sleeping Beauty and Prince Philip at the drinking fountain outside Sleeping Beauty Castle

Just outside the entrance to the Sleeping Beauty Castle attraction, guests will find a drinking fountain with a bronze statue of Sleeping beauty dancing with her prince. If you look closely, you will find the three good fairies flying around the couple keeping them safe from Maleficent.

☐ Walk through Sleeping Beauty castle to experience the story of Sleeping Beauty

As you enter the castle steps, you will climb through the tower and down the opposite side while experiencing the story of *Sleeping Beauty* the way that Disney told it in 1959.

These dioramas were created in 1955 to advertise the film *Sleeping Beauty* released four years after the opening of Disneyland. Guest could experience this fairy tale long before it came to the big screen and became a classic in the Disney archives.

This attraction was closed for many years, but was finally reopened with advanced special effects for new generations to enjoy.

Be sure to look out for the shadow of Maleficent as she hides in the shadows just before you leave the castle.

For guests unable to climb the stairs, if you look to your right as you come through the castle drawbridge, you will find a small room decorated with stately furniture fit for royalty. Within this room guests are able to experience the Sleeping Beauty attraction in full.

☐ Schedule a makeover at Bibbity Bobbity Boutique

Let the fairy godmothers wave their wand over your little one to become the latest Disney princess in this one of a kind experience. Little girls from all over the world fantasize about becoming the princesses they see on the movie screen and now Disneyland has made their dream come true. Disneyland created the Bibbity Bobbity Boutique just so every little girl can have that experience for her very own.

Bibbity Bobbity Boutique has an experience for every price range, however, for the full royal treatment, your princess will get the chance to meet her favorite princesses without having to stand in long lines at Fantasy Faire. Your party will be escorted into the royal meet and greet where your princess can get pictures with her favorite princesses throughout the day.

☐ Find the wood carvings of Captain Hook, Mr. Smee and Tick Tock Croc

On the eaves just outside of Bibbity Bobbity Boutique you need to look just above the doorway to find three carvings on the ends of the posts. These are remnants of the shop that was housed here previously. The décor was added to tie into the Peter Pan attraction just across the walkway and the shops in this area were featuring souvenirs from this classic film. Over the years, this shop has been changed, but thankfully, the imagineers decided to leave this artistic detail behind for guests to enjoy.

☐ Fly to Neverland with Peter Pan's Flight

One of the original attractions on opening day of Disneyland, Peter Pan's Flight took its cues from the 1953 animated film. The original theme for the attraction made the guest Peter Pan, flying over the rooftops of London and flying to Neverland to play with the lost boys, fight Captain Hook and celebrate with the Indians.

However, the guests did not understand the original viewpoint so the attraction was changed to include an animatronic Peter Pan in the attractions.

Board a pirate ship and fly with Wendy, Peter and Michael Darling over the rooftops of London to Neverland. There you will visit with Indians, swim with mermaids and fight Captain Hook and his band of pirates before flying home. Before your trip of over, look carefully for the lost boys hide out in the hollow tree just before your ship comes back for a landing.

☐ Try to pull the Sword from the stone

Just in front of King Arthurs Carousel you will find a large stone with a sword sticking out of the top. Once upon a time, Merlin would come into Fantasyland and pick a commoner from the crowd and they would attempt to pull the sword from the stone.

While Merlin has gone back to Camelot, the stone and the sword remains, waiting for the next king of England or for guests to pose for pictures.

☐ Ride Jingles on King Arthurs Carousel

A ride on King Arthurs Carousel is a treat all on its own, but riding the lead horse, Jingles, can add a little more magic to your ride.

This antique carousel was built in 1875 and used in Toronto, Canada, Disney bought the carousel due to its similarity to the carousel at Griffith Park where he would watch his daughters play on daddy daughter day each Sunday.

Imagineers refurbished the carousel and installed it at the center of Fantasyland for the opening in 1955 and the attractions has been thrilling children of all ages since.

Jingles was selected as the lead horse on this antique carousel. You will notice Jingles has an elaborate halter very different from the other horses. On April 8, 2008, this horse was dedicated to Disney legend, Julie Andrews to commemorate her years of service to Disney films. Look closely at the saddle decorations and you will see small paintings from *Mary Poppins*.

☐ Stop and listen to the Pearly Band entertain guests of Fantasyland

With their brightly colored costumes, the Pearly Band stepped right out of a chalk painting from *Mary Poppins* to entertain you during your time in Fantasyland. Watch as this talented group sometimes ride King Arthurs Carousel or wander the streets to include passersby's in their songs.

☐ Watch for the Evil Queen looking down at you from her tower high above the Snow White's Scary Adventures attraction

As you wander through Fantasyland, stop for a moment in front of Snow White's Scary Adventure and look up at the large ornate window. You will see the heavy drapes open to reveal the evil queen in all her splendor glaring down at you from above.

☐ Touch the golden apple sitting on the pedestal outside Snow White's Scary Adventures

As you enter the queue for Snow White's Scary Adventure, you will notice a large brass book sitting atop a pedestal and a brass apple standing silently as guest pass by. If you touch the apple you will hear the old hag cackle at you. Those in the know can startle guests as they stand in the line waiting for their time to visit with Snow White and her friends.

☐ Ride on Snow White's Scary Adventures

Another of the attractions premiering at Disneyland on opening day, Snow White's Scary Adventure, takes guest on a first-person ride through the 1937 film, *Snow White and the Seven Dwarfs*.

The original attraction became confusing for guests when they would not find the princess Snow White in the attraction. The original concept being that the guest would be the princess and go through the adventures through the eyes of Snow White.

In 1983, during a refurbishment of Fantasyland, the imagineers added Snow White to the attraction and included an elaborate queue scene in the pillar at the entrance to this attraction.

Now, ride along with the seven dwarfs through the forest and into the castle of the Evil Queen as you save Snow White from the clutches of her evil plan.

☐ Find Tinkerbell within the mine at Snow White's Scary Adventure

As you travel through Snow White's Scary Adventure, you will find some of your favorite fairy tale characters around you but there is one of your favorite fairies hiding within the seven dwarves mine.

As you enter the mine, you will see a small passage to your right with a mine cart at the entrance. If you look to the rear of this shaft, you will find a tiny Tinkerbell within this part of the mine. It come by very quickly so do not be disappointed if you cannot find her the first time you attempt to see her.

☐ Ride along with Pinocchio's Daring Journey

Pinocchio's Daring Journey came to Disneyland in 1983 when Fantasyland underwent a complete overhaul and the Mickey Mouse Club Theater was removed. The attraction, modeled after the 1940 film *Pinocchio*, takes guests through the world of the little wooden puppet and his conscience, Jiminy Cricket.

Find out what happens to the little wooden puppet when he joins Stomboli's travelling show. Will he be able to escape from pleasure island after his friend Lampwick becomes a donkey? Will Jiminy Cricket and the Blue Fairy be able to save him from Monstro the whale? All of Pinocchio's adventures are just inside the doors of this charming cottage.

☐ Get a snack at the Red Rose Tavern

Join Belle, Gaston and the Beast in the Red Rose Tavern. Inside you will not only find great food, including the delicious grey stuff, but you will find authentic props from the live *Beauty and the Beast* film.

Look at the shelves above you around the restaurant to find Lumiere, Cogsworth and Mrs. Potts, the servants of Beast. Be sure to get a picture of the elaborate stained glass of Belle and her prince before you finish your visit to this delightful village cafe.

☐ Ride on the Casey Junior Circus Train

There are only a handful of attraction still in operation since the opening of Disneyland on July 17, 1955 and Casey Junior Circus Train is one of them.

The attraction, based on the 1940 film, *Dumbo*, was designed to take guests on a short trip on the little circus train that carried the animals from city to city performing in the circus.

Ride along with your engineer Casey Junior as you travel through the hillside of Storybook Land Canal Boats. Choose to be a monkey or a lion when you choose which cage you ride in. Perhaps you just want to ride in the caboose.

Chime in when you reach the hill as you hear Casey Jr. say, "I think I can, I think I can."

☐ Fly along with Dumbo the Flying Elephant

The original ride for Dumbo the Flying Elephant opened one month after Disneyland premiered in 1955. Originally the ride was found at the furthest end of Fantasyland near the Casey Junior Circus Train. With the 1983 refurbishment of Fantasyland, Dumbo was moved to its current location and Skull Rock was removed.

A little unknown story of this attraction was the original attraction was to have pink elephants reminiscent of the Pink Elephants on Parade song in the original film. Disney vetoed the design, wanting guests to experience the ride in an innocent light.

Now you can fly with Dumbo high above Fantasyland as the little elephant with the big ears shows you how high he can go. High above, you will see his friend Timothy Mouse and Mr. Stork as you circle round and round.

☐ Get your picture taken with Dumbo the Flying Elephant

Towards the rear of the Dumbo attraction you will find a ride car waiting for guests to snap pictures for their photo album. Take your time getting the perfect shot within this classic Disney character at this beloved ride.

Nearby, you will find a calliope playing music for the guests I this area. If you look in the windows, you will see this working calliope with its many instruments working together in perfect harmony.

☐ Ride Mr. Toad's Wild Ride

Another of the attraction's guests enjoyed on the opening day of Disneyland was Mr. Toad's Wild Ride. This attraction takes guests on the wild ride from the original film *The Adventures of Ichabod and Mr. Toad*. Also known as *The Wind in the Willows*, starring Mr. Toad, Rat, Mole, McBadger and Cyril helping Mr. Toad keeping his home from being taken over by Winky and the weasels.

Now you can jump in Mr. Toads horseless carriage ad ride through Toad Hall before riding through the countryside and terrorizing the town. Keep your eye on the road or you just might fall into the harbor or even go head to head against a train.

Buckle up for your adventures with Mr. Toad and all of his friends.

☐ Join the Mad Hatter for a ride in a teacup on The Mad Tea Party

Follow the musical strains throughout Fantasyland that lead you to The Mad Tea Party. Hop in the biggest teacup you have ever seen to go spinning around the table in time to your favorite tunes from *Alice in Wonderland*.

For those looking for a bigger thrill, see just a fast you can make your teacup spin.

☐ Find one of the last remaining ticket booths existing in Disneyland at Alice in Wonderland

Standing outside the Alice in Wonderland attraction in Fantasyland you will find a large yellow mushroom with an enormous storybook on the top.

At the opening of Disneyland in 1955 through 1982 when the tickets were retired to make way for the modern all access tickets. With the retirement of these A-E tickets, the ticket booths found in various places throughout the theme park were retired also.

This yellow mushroom remains as a memorial to these booths and a distinctive entrance to this beloved attraction.

☐ Ride in a giant caterpillar and down the rabbit hole with Alice in Wonderland

Opening in 1958, Alice in Wonderland was much different than the current ride fans enjoy. The original attraction had many rooms that were more disturbing than enchanting and the ride went through a major overhaul in 1983 to the version you now see.

Now, follow the footsteps of the White Rabbit and travel to the wonderous place called Wonderland. Find Tweedle Dee and Tweedle Dum, sing with the flowers and avoid that rascal the Cheshire Cat before your end up in the garden of the Queen of Hearts.

Run for your life as she yells, "Off with their head!" Lastly, join the mad tea party before it is time to leave madness behind.

☐ Step in the Mad Hatter shop and get your favorite Disneyland hat

Inside this little shop, you will find every type of hat known in Disneyland. While you are trying on, make sure you take a peek at the bunny house on the second floor. If you look in the mirror you might even find one of the characters from Alice in Wonderland peeking back at you before he disappears again.

Before you go, take a peek in the window and see the tea party awaiting Alice and her friends from Wonderland.

☐ Find the door to the White Rabbits house

Just outside The Mad Hatter shop you will find a small door. The brass plaque reads, W Rabbit. You have come upon the house of the White Rabbit from Alice in Wonderland.

Be sure to get a picture of this little-known feature of Fantasyland.

☐ Get a picture with The Cheshire Cat resting next to the Alice in Wonderland attraction.

Quietly watching over Fantasyland, you will find The Cheshire Cat with his ever-present grin looking down at you, waiting for you to take a picture with this famous cat.

If you look just above the Cheshire Cat, you will find two birds with hammer heads that have escaped the Tulgy Woods within this attraction.

☐ Stop at the restroom next to Alice in Wonderland.

While there are many bathrooms throughout Disneyland resort, the stalls at this particular one may be just a little more whimsical.

Inside this bathroom, the Queen of Hearts has been busy decorating with each door a different card in her deck. Also note the stained-glass light fixtures. The queen left her mark on this quiet corner of Fantasyland.

☐ Visit Tinker Bell and her friends at Pixie Hollow

Shrink down to the size of a pixie to find the entrance to Pixie Hollow where Tinker Bell, Iridessa, Silvermist, Rosetta and even her sister Periwinkle live in this enchanted place.

On your way, don't miss the little houses where fairies live along the path. In the evening, this area glows with the special pixie dust from the fairies to create mesmerizing colors throughout the flowers.

☐ Find the plaster cast of the yeti footprint at the Matterhorn

Go on an exploration to find the plaster cast of a footprint left behind by a yeti. It is rumored that the yeti is still within the snowcapped peak of the Matterhorn.

Explorers found this incredible footprint and brought back a cast as proof of the gigantic creature living within the icy slope of the Matterhorn mountain.

☐ Ride on a toboggan through the Matterhorn

Fly though the snow on a run-away toboggan trying to escape the clutches of the yeti that haunts this mountain. Ride through ice caverns and water falls of melting ice as the yeti will attempt to capture you.

The first of the Disneyland mountain range, you can still see climbers from time to time scaling the top of this famous mountain. At night, you will see Tinker Bell flying from the top of the Matterhorn to Sleeping Beauty Castle as she spreads her special magic throughout the Magic Kingdom.

Notice the large holes at the top of this mountain? This is all that is left of the Skyway attraction that brought guests from Fantasyland to Tomorrowland and back again, flying high above the attractions.

An interesting bit of trivia about Matterhorn is the half-court basketball court within this mountain. That is correct, cast members have been known to get a game of basketball together within the Matterhorn mountain.

☐ Sing along with the children of the world on It's a Small World

Join the happiest cruise in all of Disneyland as you travel the nations of the world singing this anthem to good will, It's a Small World After All. Look closely for your favorite Disney characters to be singing along in their countries.

Premiering May 30, 1966, Walt Disney created a gala event with children pouring water from all of the oceans of the world into the canal of this attraction to bring all the waters of the world together. It was Walt Disney's dream to bring people together in the same way with his theme park and this is the theme of this enchanting attraction.

Do not miss this attraction during the holidays when you can see the world transformed to a winter wonderland with a new song for you to sing along with.

☐ Watch the clock chime at It's a Small World

The clock on the façade of It's a Small World is not just another decoration that moves randomly. This clock face is an actual working clock that chimes every fifteen minutes with dolls representing the children of the world that come out to march around the It's a Small World attraction.

Listen as the clock chimes the hour and minute and the large doors open to reveal the clock that helps you to know the time in a very creative way.

☐ Watch Mickey's Magical Map at the Fantasyland Theater

Join Mickey as he is apprentice to the map maker. Watch the mischief he gets into and the friends he meets along the way as he follows the map to new undiscovered places. Sing along with King Louie, Pocahontas, Stitch and many others of your favorite Disney characters as they sing your favorite songs.

In the end, will Mickey finish the map for Yensid or will he fail his master as he did in *Fantasia*?

☐ Find another of the last remaining ticket booths at Disneyland

At the entrance to the Storybook Land Canal Boat you will find a small lighthouse standing tall at the entrance to the dock for the Storybook Land attraction.

This lighthouse is another of the elusive ticket booths that sold the A through E tickets on Disneyland's opening day. The tickets were retired in the 1980's to make way for the all access tickets but these adorable booths remain.

☐ Travel on the waterways of the Storybookland Canal Boats

Travel through the mouth of Monstro the whale to a land never seen in your world. See miniatures of your favorite Disney films come to life with a little bit of pixie dust. From *Alice in Wonderland* to *The Three Little Pigs*, you will see their world as you travel the canal of Storybook Land Canal Boats.

Find the lamp in the cave of wonders or the pumpkin coach from Cinderella. Not a detail is missed throughout the best love stories of your childhood.

☐ Watch Monstro the whale's blow hole shoot water into the air as wink at you

Monstro the whale leads guests from Fantasyland to Storybook land but he is still watching guests as they spend time in Fantasyland. You can watch Monstro wink at passerby's and breathe through his blow hole during your time in Fantasyland.

# Toontown

Travel to the home of your favorite Disney characters as you step into the city limits of Toontown.

Opening in 1993, Toontown was inspired by the film *Who Framed Roger Rabbit* in which the toons live in their own animated world adjacent to downtown Hollywood in the 1930's.

The architecture of Toontown challenged imagineers to build an entire city with no right angles. While the homes have been updated throughout the years, this area holds the whimsy of your favorite animation come to life.

Find Roger Rabbit and help him save his wife Jessica through the streets of Toontown but be careful or you might get dipped. Stop in at the Laugh Factory, get an ice-cold treat from Clarabelle's and visit the most famous mouse in the world.

Before you go on your way, be sure you visit the homes of Donald, Goofy and Minnie, you may even see them strolling through the streets of Toontown.

☐ Stop to read the Toontown landmark 3 ½ sign as you enter Toontown

This dedication plaque at the entrance to Toontown is passed over by many guests in their excitement to being their time in Toontown. For those who take the time, you will find this little gem very amusing.

Stop to read this sign with the famous Toontown quote, "Laughter is sunshine you can hear."

☐ Get a cold treat at Freeze Time

Parked on the streets of Toontown you will find a small trailer with lots of sporting equipment attached to the outside. Get an ice-cold frozen drink here to sip while you wander through this magical land.

You may recognize this trailer from the Mickey Mouse cartoon *Mickeys Trailer*. Mickey, Donald and Goofy travel through the mountains in this little trailer to find all sorts of trouble.

The sporting equipment is a nod to the Goofy cartoon's, *Hockey Homicide*, *How to Play Football*, *How to Play Golf* and *The Art of Skiing*.

Take some time to cool off and enjoy this nostalgic little trailer.

☐ Visit the Toontown park

In a quiet, shady corner of Toontown stand Toontown park. This tiny park is the perfect hideaway for those who need a break. Put your feet up and enjoy the sights and sounds around you before continuing on your way through Toontown.

☐ Find the nod to famed Disney imaginer Marty Sklar in Goofy's pumpkin patch.

Marty Sklar may not be a name instantly recognizable to guests visiting Disneyland, but he has been responsible for more Disney magic than you realize.

Sklar was responsible for the It's a Small World attraction for the World's Fair in 1964. Later, Sklar became the vice-president of planning for the Walt Disney World resort. Sklar also was one of the creative designers for Disneyland Paris, Tokyo Disney, Disney's Animal Kingdom and Disney-MGM Studios.

In 2001, Sklar was named a Disney legend and, in 2006, Sklar became the International Ambassador of Walt Disney Imagineering.

This pumpkin with the likeness of Sklar is a small dedication to the work of this great man.

☐ Ride on the Toontown Trolley

Traveling through Toontown is the little red Toontown Trolley. Like everything else in Toontown, this little street car meanders down the road wobbling along the way.

☐ Play in Goofy's Playhouse

Goofy's house, like Goofy himself, is full of odd things, both inside and out. Before you enter Goofy's house, be sure to walk through his garden and see some of the strange vegetables he is growing.

Walk through his house and see how Goofy built his house. At Goofy's, feel free to jump on furniture and play to your heart's content. Be sure to play a tune on his piano before you leave.

☐ Visit Donald Duck's boat

Hop aboard the boat of Donald Duck and see how this crazy duck lives. Be sure to climb to the upper deck to get a duck's eye view of Toontown. Climb down the cargo net or spend some time as the captain before Donald gets home.

☐ Check out Gadget's Go Coaster and see how this ingenious chipmunk has built her attraction

> Gadget, a friend of Chip and Dale, has been busy at work building Gadget's Go Coaster.
>
> As you walk through the queue, you will find match sticks, rubber bands, and even a toothbrush have been used for the rails along the queue.
>
> As you get to the house, drinking straws make up the rain gutters, dominoes are used for the doors and a pink eraser is used for the pedestal for the cast member. notice the blue prints by the Chinny Chin Chin construction company before you take a ride on your acorn coaster.

☐ Visit Chip and Dales treehouse

> Hidden in Toontown is this little gem. Chip and Dale have their own acorn treehouse in a quiet corner for them to enjoy. A wonderful place to rest or just enjoy at your leisure.

☐ Play a tune at the Toontown fountain

> A focal point of the neighborhood in Toontown is the fountain with several musical instruments adorning the center. If you look at the ground around this fountain, you will notice several round discs.

Feel free to step on these and join in the music next time you visit Toontown.

☐ Visit the home of Mickey Mouse

Walk through Mickeys home and see his memorabilia from years in the film business. Listen to his messages and read his cork board as you wander through the livingroom. Stop to listen to his player piano and sit in his Family room to watch classic cartoons.

Need to do a load of laundry? Step into Mickey's laundry room where he is fully stocked but there might be a load in his washing machine.

Stepping into Mickeys back yard and see if you can catch that pesky gopher in Mickey's garden.

The highlight of your day will be to visit Mickey's movie barn where you will see props from Mickey's most famous films.

Before you get to meet the mouse himself, watch some of Mickey's work on the screen. Top off you day with a meet and greet with Mickey in his dressing room.

☐ Stop by the house of Mickey's best girl, Minnie Mouse

See how the first lady of Disneyland lives as you walk through her lovely little house.

Take a peek at the magazine draped over the arm of Minnie's chair in her living room before stopping in Minnie's dressing room to read Minnie's email and fix your makeup in her vanity mirror.

Check in Minnie's kitchen to make sure her cake doesn't fall and have tea and cookies. Read she shopping list on the front of her refrigerator and open the door to see how Minnie eats when she is hungry.

Step out into the garden to meet Minnie and have tea with this famous mouse.

☐ Visit the Toontown post office and turn the knobs on the post office boxes to hear the voices of your favorite Toontown residents

The clerk in the post office seems to be out, but the mail is waiting for the famous Toontown residents. Turn the knob for Roger Rabbit, Jessica Rabbit, Mickey Mouse and all the rest as you listen to messages left just for you.

Notice that Goofy's box is a little different from the rest. You might even hear different messages if you turn the knobs more than once.

☐ Open the Toontown Mailbox

Toontown residents might find themselves with a surprise when they open the mailbox on the street in front of the post office. Listen for a voice telling you to close the door or other various scolding's.

It might be challenging getting you mail delivered with a mailbox like the one in Toontown.

☐ Ring the doorbell on the Camera Shop in Toontown

Ring the doorbell for the Camera Shop, but you might want to smile and say cheese before you do.

☐ Ring the doorbell of the Toontown dog pound to hear it meow at you

The Toontown dog pound is not like any other. Be sure to pose for a picture of you behind the bars but you might notice they might not hold you in.

☐ Try the barbell on the streets of Toontown

For guests looking to improve your physique, try the barbell o the streets of Toontown but do not be surprised if the bar is a little stretchy. This comical barbell is just another of the surprises that await you in Toontown.

☐ Get a sweet treat at Clarabelle's

Clarabelle, one of the original characters from the mind of Walt Disney may not be one of the more recognizable stars of animated shorts, but she has her own shop in Toontown.

Do not miss a chance for a sweet treat at this adorable shop.

☐ Find the talking drinking fountain in Toontown

Everything in Toontown is not what is appears. Next door to Clarabelle's is the only talking drinking fountain around.

Be sure to sip more than once to hear this fountain's variety of sound effects before you are done quenching your thirst.

☐ Read the windows in Toontown and find the Laugh O'Gram Films window

Throughout Toontown you will find businesses that will tickle your funny bone. You can get sound business advise from none other than Scrooge Mc Duck, keep your money safe at the Third Little Piggy bank or gets singing lessons from Clara Cluck.

Hidden in a corner of Toontown is the window for Laugh O'Gram Films Inc. Found next to the Toontown Skool, this window make now be noticeable from anywhere else around Toontown.

When Walt Disney was just twenty years old, he created his first animation studio. It was this studio that created Disney's first real cartoon, *Little Red Riding Hood*. Disney, along with his animators, Ub Iwerks, Fritz Freleng, Carman Maxwell and Hugh Harman would create new characters like Julius the Cat and the pilot for the Alice Comedies in this tiny animation studios.

Toontown pays tribute to this piece of Disney history with a small window.

☐ Walk through the backstage area and alleys of Toontown in the queue of Roger Rabbits Cartoon Spin

Enter the garage for the Toontown cab company and take a walk through the dark streets of Toontown. Read some of the license plates from some of the Toontown residents hanging just inside the door before traversing the dark streets of Toontown.

Knock of the door of the Ink and Paint Club and try to tell the bouncer the right password to gain access to this private club.

Go back stage at the theater and find Jessica Rabbits dressing room. Read some of the notices on the call board before heading into the alley behind to find the secret hideout of the weasels and where they make the dip.

Find the crates from the Toy Boat Toy Boat Toy Boat company before boarding your cab to star your adventure.

☐ Ride Roger Rabbits Cartoon Spin

Ride with Bennie the Cab to find and save Jessica Rabbit from the weasels. Travel through this crazy world where the rules don't apply. Watch out for the Bullina China Shop and don't get electrocuted when you travel through the Toontown electric company.

Don't get dizzy as you fall from the heights and land in the Laugh Factory just in time to save Jessica and avoid getting dipped.

☐ Find the Toontown insurance company

Being a toon is so dangerous, the need for an insurance company is necessary in Toontown. Finding this insurance office is pretty simple, just find the large safe that has crashed into the sidewalk outside the Roger Rabbit Cartoon Spin and you are there.

Be sure to read the door to see how many different types of insurance they sell.

☐ Get your picture in front of the Toontown fountain

Another of the decorative fountains in Toontown stands near the entrance to Roger Rabbit's Cartoon Spin. Be sure to get your picture in front of this fun monument to Roger Rabbit's driving skills.

☐ Get pictures with your favorite residents of Toontown

Keep an eye out throughout your day in Toontown and you just might find your favorite characters walking along the streets to get pictures and autographs.

Goofy and Pluto can be found nearby Roger Rabbit's Cartoon Spin, while Chip and Dale might be found near their treehouse.

Don't miss this great chance to get some pictures with the whole Toontown gang.

☐ Test the plunger at the Toontown Fireworks Factory, you may just set off the fireworks if you are not careful

Just across from Roger Rabbits Cartoon Spin you will find the Toontown Fireworks Factory. This poor building has been through an explosion or two in its time.

Try your hand at the plunger and see what results. Is it a firework show or a dud?

☐ Find the Dalmatian puppy at the Toontown Fire Department

Pose for pictures in the Toontown firetruck but you might be watched while you do.

Look high up in the top window of the fire station and you may see a small puppy peeking at you before he ducks back inside. If you want to see the puppy for yourself, just ring the doorbell on the Firehouse and hurry back to see this adorable puppy.

☐ Open some of the boxes near the Glass Company to hear the contents come to life

Deliveries in Toontown are very different from anywhere else. Try lifting some of the lids on the crates near the Glass company. You will laugh when you hear what is inside these boxes waiting for their owners.

Whether it is a box of laughter or a train whistle, be sure to try these crates for yourself.

☐ Open the doors to the Toontown Electric Company

> Just like the other buildings around Toontown, the Electric Company is not what it appears to be. Open the door and you may get more than you bargained for as the electricity greets you at the door.

☐ Listen to the police telephone near the Glass Factory in Toontown

> The police telephone stands on the street for anyone who happens by to pick up the receiver. Listen to the police giving orders or maybe just being silly toons.

☐ Spend some time in The Gag Factory to see what's inside

> High up on the shelves of the Gag Factory, you might find some props from your favorite Disney cartoons.
>
> Look for a box for W. Giant with the singing harp within. A box of one liners ready for the next joke. Directly above you, watch the conveyor belt bringing gags by the dozen out ready for sale.

# Star Wars: Galaxy's Edge

Join the rebel forces as you enter this outpost on the edge of the galaxy. Fly along with your crew on the Millennium Falcon or join the resistance to rise up to fight for your freedom.

Build your lightsaber weapon or your new droid before finding your new jedi robe in the marketplace.

For Jedi's looking for sustenance on their long journey, stop at Docking Bay 7 or pick up a blue milk for the long road ahead.

*Warning, there are spoilers to the attractions and films within this chapter. Please be aware of this before reading about the areas contains in Star Wars: Galaxy's Edge.*

☐ Walk through the tunnel to Batuu

> While the mountain range of Batuu is visible from the Rivers of America, the entrance to Star Wars:

Galaxy's Edge is completely hidden from the rest of Disneyland.

As you walk down the path and through the tunnel, the world of Batuu comes alive before your eyes. The imagineers have created a way to bring guests the thrill of experiencing this land as if they were landing on a far distant outpost of space.

Now it is time for you to experience Batuu for yourself.

- [ ] Get your picture taken in front of the First Order TIE Echelon

    This twin ion engine shuttle is the perfect backdrop for your pictures while on Batuu. Be sure to stop and get pictures in front of this impressive First Order transport before it takes off for another mission.

- [ ] Read the signs around Batuu

    Aurebesh is the official language of Batuu and those visiting will notice that most of the signs around this outpost are written in this language.

    While the alphabet of Batuu is not posted anywhere on the outpost, guests can download the Disneyland app and translate the signage to understand these signs and store names into your language.

☐ Learn the phrases spoken on Batuu

> The citizens of Batuu will greet travelers with phrases that may not be recognizable to guests visiting for the first time. But you will get to know the greetings very quickly.
>
> Learning these phrases is very simple, but there are some that are secret codes to ensure that the First Order does not discover your allegiance.
>
> Ignite the spark—this is a resistance greeting
>
> Light the fire—the response to Ignite the spark
>
> In no time, you will be speaking like a native with the citizens of Batuu.

☐ Try the blue or green milk

> Any fans of the Star Wars films remember when Luke Skywalker walked into the cantina and they caught their first glimpse of the blue milk. Many years later, we watched Luke drink green milk after milking the female Latha-Siren.
>
> Now guests of Batuu can sample these for themselves at the outdoor vending area.

☐ Enjoy a beverage at Oga's Cantina

Travelers can stop for a cool beverage at Oga's Cantina, a cantina similar to Mos Eisley Cantina as seen in *Star Wars A New Hope*.

Now travelers can step up to the bar or sit in a secluded table to enjoy a variety of alcoholic and non-alcoholic beverages served throughout the day on Batuu.

☐ Enjoy the music of D.J. R-3X at Oga's Cantina

While in Oga's Cantina, you will listen to the sounds of D.J. R-3X and this little droid should look familiar to anyone who has visited Tomorrowland over the years. This droid is actually Rex from Star Tours. Rex was your pilot on the Starspeeder 3000 for years and now has a new purpose at Oga's Cantina.

☐ Watch as the hyper drive malfunctions during your time at Oga's Cantina

Every so often, the hyper drive that powers Oga's Cantina will stop working. The lights dim and the music will stop until the staff can get the hyper drive working once more.

☐ Find the Ewok spear beer tap

> If you look behind the bar at Oga's, you will find a familiar Ewok spear head with the Yub Nub beer. Fans of *Star Wars Return of the Jedi* will recognize this beer name is also the song the Ewok's sing in this classic film.
>
> Guests may recognize many of the other items behind the bar that have been scavenged from the vast reachs of the universe.

☐ Find Ponda Baba's arm behind the bar at Oga's Cantina

> Fans of Star Wars a New Hope will remember when Luke Skywalker was saved from Pondo Baba by Obi Wan Kenobi in the cantina. Now guests can find a drawing of his arm on one of the jars behind the bar of Oga's Cantina.

☐ Get your picture with the Millennium Falcon

> The focal point of Batuu is the Millennium Falcon docked on this outpost. Guests can now get their picture with this infamous smuggler ship during their time on Batuu.
>
> Be sure to get this perfect memory of your time on this outpost with a picture with the Millennium Falcon.

☐ Find the Sabacc game in the queue for Millennium Falcon: Smugglers Run

As guests enter the queue for the Millenium Falcon: Smugglers Run, you will notice an area directly behind the falcon with a small hexagon shaped table. If you look clsely, the cards sitting atop this table are the exact cards used when Han Solo won the Falcon from Lando Calrissian in the film *Solo*.

☐ Find the small red droid from *Star Wars: A New Hope*

In the storage are behind the Millennium Falcon, you will find a small red droid in front of two orange jumpsuits. Guests may recognize this droid as one the Jawas were trying to sell in the *Star Wars: A New Hope*.

☐ Find the Scout Trooper helmet used as a drip pan in the maintenance area

Hidden in the shadows just before guests make a turn to the second level, you will find a Scout Trooper helmet seen in *Star Wars: Return of the Jedi*.

The resistance clearly has a sense of humor when they repurpose these items.

*One hundred things you need to do at Disneyland before you die*

☐ Watch the sub-light engine come to life on the second level gantry

As guests make their way to the second level, you will see a very large sub-light engine being worked on. Periodically, you will see and hear this engine come to life with lights and sound showing guests that this outpost is actively working.

☐ Find Porg nests around the queue area

As you work your way through the queue towards the lounge of the Falcon, look around and see if you can find small nest hidden in corners. These are Porg nests waiting for their small inhabitants to return from exploring Batuu.

☐ Enter the lounge of the Millennium Falcon

Enter the lounge and guests will feel like they have just stepped into their favorite Star Wars films. Feel free to sit at the holochess table but be sure to let the wookie win.

Every once in a while, guests will hear and see the Falcon power down, be sure to run to the left corner and hit the large red button just in time to bring the Falcon back to life.

☐ Find the Marksman-H combat remote

If you spend any amount of time in the lounge area, you may recognize the helmet used by Luke Skywalker when he trains in *Star Wars: The Empire Strikes Back.* Leaning against this helmet is the small combat droid that Luke was attempting to block in this famous film.

☐ Join the crew of the Millennium Falcon Smuggler Run

Board the Millennium Falcon and help intercept the Coaxium to gain a healthy profit for your crew and Hondo Ohnaka. Jump to light speed and find the train with your cargo waiting for you take it for yourself.

But be careful to dodge obstacles and avoid getting caught. Once you reach the base, find out what percentage your crew will earn, less any damages of course.

☐ Find the frozen Rathtar as you exit the Millennium Falcon

As you exit your ride on the Millennium Falcon, look at the walls around you. On one wall you will find a Rathtar frozen in carbonite for all eternity. You may recall the Rathtar chasing Han Solo and

Chewy in *Star Wars: the Force Awakens* as they narrowly escape with their lives.

☐ Find the cargo ship above Docking Bay 7 Food and Cargo

High above the entrance to Docking Bay 7 Food and Cargo, you will find a cargo ship that has landed on the outpost. As you look at this ship, notice the numbers 77, 80 and 83. These number signify the years that the first three Star Wars films were released.

While you may only see two or the three on the rooftop, stop inside this restaurant to see the third being lowered from the ceiling into the cargo bay.

☐ Stop in at Docking Bay 7 Food and Cargo for a great meal

For those looking for a great meal on Batuu, stop at Docking Bay 7 during your travels. Try the Kaadu ribs with blueberry corn muffin and a cold Phattro to quench your thirst. Try the Endorian Tip Yip salad or Chilled noodle salad. Be sure to get the Batuu-bon for dessert to top off a delicious meal.

☐ Examine the trash receptacle number throughout Star Wars Galaxy's Edge

> Throughout this outpost, guests will find trash and recycle cans for their garbage. One the trash cans, notice the local writing with the number 3263827. This sign actually reads, "trash to sector 3263827". For those Star Wars fans, this is the very same area where Luke Skywalker, Han Solo and Princess Leia find themselves trapped and being slowly crushed in *Star Wars: A New Hope*.

☐ Explore Ronto Roasters and see who is cooking

> Guests getting a snack at Ronto Roasters will find a familiar droid cooking the meat. This tall droid was torturing his smaller counterparts in *Star Wars: Return of the Jedi* when C3PO and R2D2 are given to Jabba the Hut.

☐ Find the large podracer engine cooking the meat at Ronto Roasters

> The enormous blue engine is instantly recognizable to Star Wars fans. This podracer engine is cooking the meat turning on the spit at Ronto Roasters so travelers can get a hot meal.
>
> Fans of *Star Wars: The Phantom Menace* remember a young Anakin Skywalker winning the pod race. This engine came off of one of the pod racers that

was destroyed during a pod race and repurposed to serve hot food daily at the Black Spire Outpost.

☐ Taste the Outpost popcorn mix

Near Ronto's, you will find Kat Saka's Kettle, where they offer sweet and spicy popcorn for weary travelers. The red and purple give travelers a tasty treat to take with them as they explore the shopping stalls.

For those looking for something a little sweeter, try the chocolate covered popcorn.

☐ Find your Jedi attire at Black Spire Outfitters

Whether you want to dress like Rey or your favorite Sith, Black Spire outfitters offer everything a Jedi needs to be ready for battle. From shirts to vests to arm wraps to robes, these high-quality clothing items are just perfect for the traveler exploring the Black Spire Outpost.

Be warned, travelers over the age of fourteen will not be able to don their new robes while at the Disneyland resort. Little travelers will be permitted to dress as long as robes do not drag the ground.

☐ Visit Toydarian Toy Maker

Zabaka the toy makers has been hard at work making toys for travelers visiting the Black Spire Outpost. Stop in to find plush toys and puzzles to keep you entertained during your long travels through Batuu.

If you look above, you will find many tributes to your favorite Star Wars moments. Above the cash register area, guests will find Darth Vader and Obi Wan Kenobi locked in a battle to the death. Nearby, the Millennium Falcon is racing through space chased by the empire and Jabba the Hutt's sailing barge sits high on one of the shelves.

Be sure to watch the silhouette of Zabaka through the frosted glass busy at work on his next creation before you continue through the stalls.

☐ Find Watto from the Phantom Menace

Just outside Toydarian Toy Maker, you will see a sign with a small green creature. Fans of *Star Wars: The Phantom Menace* will recognize Watto, the owner of Shmi and Anakin Skywalker on the sign.

☐ Visit Creature Stall for your new pet

Find adorable creatures from all over the galaxy at the Creature Stall on Batuu. For some travelers, the

Wampa is their creature of choice. For others, the cuddly loth cat is more their choice.

Be sure to look through all the creatures up for adoption but do not miss the creatures high above in their cages. If you look closely at the cages with the tags, you may see glowing eyes peering out at you from the depths of their cage.

Ask the proprietor about adopting today.

☐ Find Han Solo's landspeeder from the film *Solo*

As you explore the stalls in the market, you will come across a small rack with three landspeeders. The blue speeder on the bottom once belonged to Han Solo in the film *Solo*. Be sure to get a picture of this miniature version of this famous landspeeder.

☐ Visit the Droid Depot for your new mechanical friend

This small shop offers guests a once in a lifetime experience. Step up to the conveyor belt and pick the parts of your droid as they roll by. Once you've selected the perfect pieces, take them to the assembly area and you now have your own working droid to take home. Once you have your new friend, he will be placed in a handy carrying vessel to make transporting this little droid easier.

☐ Find the imperial enforcer droid from *Rouge 1* within the Droid Depot

Within the many cages in Droid Depot, you will find one containing a large grey headless droid. Some make recognize this as K-2SO from the film *Rouge 1*.

☐ Find the remains of the Imperial probe droid outside the Droid Depot

As you exit the Droid Depot, look at the junk area in the rear. Hanging in this area is an Imperial Probe Droid that has seen better days. Fans may recognize this as the droid that was looking for the rebels in *Star Wars: The Empire Strikes Back.* Since its first appearance, this droid has been seen in various incarnations of the Star Wars universe.

☐ Explore the collection within Dok-Ondar's Den of Antiquities

Travelers from every galaxy come to Dok-Ondar's Den of Antiquities to find treasures only seen on the movie screens. Masks, collectibles, lightsabers and Kyber Crystals. As you wander through this shop, Busts of your favorite Jedi or Sith can be purchased. Kyber Crystals will glow for you when you configure them correctly or Jedi gear including patches for your robes.

☐ Find the golden head of Jar Jar Binks among the upper level collection

Among the vast number of items on the second level, a golden head of Jar Jar Binks can be found atop a box waiting for the perfect travelers to take home.

☐ Admire the Medal of Bravery at Dok-Ondar's Den of Antiquities

High above, hanging on the wall behind the main counter, you will find the very medal presented to Luke Skywalker and Han Solo in *Star Wars: A New Hope*. Get a picture of this amazing medal before your time in Dok-Ondar's is complete.

☐ Marvel at the taxidermy animals in Dok-Ondar's

Several exotic animal heads can be found within Dok-Ondar's Den of Antiquities. Guests may recognize the Tauntaun and the Nexu from the Star Wars universe among the various creatures displayed.

☐ Find the taxidermy Wampa on the second level of Dok-Ondar's

The large white animal standing on the second level is very intimidating, but do not be afraid. This Wampa is the very creature that attacked Luke

Skywalker on the frozen planet of Hoth in *Star Wars: the Empire Strikes Back* and now he is on display for travelers looking for the very unique.

☐ Create your own light saber within Savi's Workshop

Join in this ancient Jedi ritual of building your own light saber within Savi's workshop.

This secretive ceremony offers travelers a chance to create their custom light sabers complete with activation ceremony. Then slide your new weapon in the custom sleeve to carry with you as you explore the rest of the outpost.

☐ Find the landspeeder from *Star Wars a New Hope*

In a far end of the Black Spire outpost, you will find a garage with several vehicles waiting for maintenance. One of these vehicles is familiar to fans of *Star Wars: a New Hope*. The Landspeeder Luke Skywalker and Obi Wan Kenobi travel in to Mos Eisley Spaceport.

☐ Interact with the Stormtroopers as they interrogate travelers

As you wander through Batuu be on the lookout for Stormtroopers interrogating guests. These stormtroopers are looking for a member of the resistance Vi Moradi and you may even see them chasing this elusive member of the resistance through the streets of Batuu.

Stay on your best behavior or they may detain you for questioning.

☐ Watch out for Kylo Ren looking for members of the resistance

The infamous Kylo Ren is personally looking for members of the resistance throughout the First Order encampment. You may find the son of Han Solo near Docking Bay 7 with his Stormtroopers keeping him safe.

Be sure to avoid interrogation as he may detain you if he suspects you know something about the resistance.

☐ Find Chewbacca around the resistance base towards the mountain outpost

Chewbacca can be found nearby the Rise of the Resistance to pose for pictures and interact with travelers looking to join the resistance. The loveable Wookie loves posing with guests while he wanders through the back roads of the Black Spire Outpost.

☐ Interact with Rey around the Rise of the Resistance area

   Rey is traveling the back roads nearby Rise of the Resistance posing for pictures and signing autographs with travelers. Be sure to stop if you happen to see this new generation of Jedi warrior during your travels through Batuu.

☐ Watch Chewbacca and the resistance fixing the X-wing fighter near Rise of the Resistance

   Travelers navigating the road around Rise of the Resistance may find Chewbacca and several members of the resistance trying to fix one of the X-wing fighters in the evenings. Be sure to take some time to watch them argue and work on this fighter during your time on Batuu.

☐ Ride Rise of the Resistance

   The resistance is looking for new members and it is your turn to join them to assist in defeating the First Order.

   Traverse the hidden passageways within the mountain and travel to the secret base. Be careful so you do not become prisoners on a Star Destroyer. If you find yourself the prisoner of the First Order, cooperate and do not give away the secrets of the rebels.

# Frontierland

Step back to the origins of the United States as you enter Frontierland. Walk through the gates of a frontier fort and learn about the sacrifice and determination of the settlers who formed the country we know today.

Along your travels, join in a show at the Golden Horseshoe or try your hand at some fancy shooting at the Exposition Shooting Gallery.

Travel on an authentic paddleboat around the Rivers of America or ride through the wilderness on a runaway mine train. Top off your time in Frontierland with an authentic Mexican meal and dessert at the Golden Horseshoe as you watch the residents of Frontierland perform for you live on stage.

☐ Find the award to Walt Disney from the American Humane Society

> Disney never wanted Disneyland to be about himself, but he was awarded many commendations throughout his life.
>
> At the entrance to Frontierland at the base of the flagpole, you will find a plaque acknowledging Disney's Humane efforts throughout the world. While most guests walk right by this small plaque, it is another recognition to the kind of man Walt Disney was.

☐ Stop off at the Shooting Exposition and try your hand at some good old fashion shooting gallery fun

> Get your tokens and try shooting at the targets to bring them to life. While you're playing, read some of the epitaphs on the headstones in the boot hill cemetery. Fire at the sky to see ghost riders fly through the night.
>
> Be sure to try this game of skill during your time in Frontierland.

☐ Notice the wheel ruts and cowboy boot prints in the path

> Along the walkways of Frontierland, you will notice the remnants of previous Frontierland residents.

Horse shoe prints, cowboy boots and cover wagon wheel ruts can be found in the pathways as you walk through the quaint town from centuries past.

☐ Try some authentic Mexican food at Rancho De Zocalo in Frontierland

Visit this Mexican villa complete with fountains and colorful tiles as you enjoy Carnitas, burritos and taco salads. Enjoy this Al fresco dining experience while tasting what chefs have been preparing for you.

Be sure to stop by during Halloween to see the corn husk garland and Dia de los Muertos decorations surrounding you while you enjoy your meal.

☐ Take a stroll into Pioneer Mercantile and find the marionette of Sheriff Woody

Bypassed by most guests to the Pioneer Mercantile, you will find this marionette of Sheriff Woody waiting to dance to tunes from Toy Story. *You've got a Friend in Me* will play as you make him dance.

This old-fashioned marionette love to entertain guest on their travels throughout Frontierland.

☐ Watch Frontierland cartoons on the movie screen in Pioneer Mercantile

Stop during your shopping trip and watch classic western cartoons from the heyday of Disney animation. Not only short subjects, but scenes from *Home on the Range* and *Pocahontas* can be seen while you find the perfect souvenir.

☐ Find the hidden safe and ask the cast members for a sneak peek at what is inside

Within the shops of the Pioneer Mercantile you will find an old fashion safe to keep the money from desperados. This safe is behind the counter to keep it safe, but, if you answer the question right, you may get a sneak peek.

☐ Listen to the nickelodeon in the Pioneer Mercantile

Within the Pioneer Mercantile is another antique nickelodeon. Listen to the strains of music coming from this engineering wonder as it plays the various instruments in perfect rhythm.

☐ Find the heroes of the American frontier on the walls of Pioneer Mercantile.

Within the shops in Frontierland, you will find original portraits of frontier legends Wild Bill

Hickok, Calamity Jane and John Wesley Hardon, some of the best-known characters of the wild west.

Disney includes these historical figures in his theme park to educate guests about where we have come from and to always remember the people who built our country.

☐ Pop into the Golden Horseshoe for a bite to eat and enjoy a rootin' tootin' show

The Golden Horseshoe has been a favorite attraction of guests since Disneyland's opening. Disney legends Wally Boag and Betty Taylor entertained audiences for decades and now a whole new generation are making guests laughs with their wild west shows.

Enjoy a yummy ice cream sundae or some fish and chips while laughing and clapping along with these talented entertainers.

☐ Admire the private box of Walt Disney within the Golden Horseshoe

Within the Golden Horseshoe, stop for a moment to look up at the private box to the left of the stage on the second floor.

This was the box of Disneyland founder Walt Disney and still remains empty in respect to Mr. Disney. Disney handpicked most of the performers at Disneyland and enjoyed popping in to the Golden Horseshoe to watch the shows. Throughout Disney's life, this box was always reserved just for him and remains a silent memorial to Disney's love for his park.

- [ ] Take some time to peruse Rainbow Ridge at Big Thunder Mesa, the small town adjacent to the tracks of the Big Thunder Mountain Railroad

   Across from the entrance to Big Thunder Mountain Railroad, you will find a small frontier town beyond the tracks.

   Included in these buildings are the hotel, saloon and mercantile. Zoom in with your camera to read the signs to see what the residents of Rainbow Ridge are doing in their town.

- [ ] Find the hidden Sleeping Beauty Castle while riding Big Thunder Mountain Railroad

   As you begin your ride on the Big Thunder Mountain Railroad you will travel through a cave with bats flying around you. As you climb the first hill with water pouring down from either side, look at the apex of this water fall. A familiar sight may be carved in the granite, Sleeping Beauty Castle has been immortalized in this attraction.

*One hundred things you need to do at Disneyland before you die*

☐ Walk the path from Frontierland to Fantasyland

> The path from Frontierland to Fantasyland has had a recent face lift and is all new for guests to experience. This area also hides the entrance to the new Star Wars area of Disneyland. Enjoy this nice walk through the quiet side of Disneyland.

☐ Stop between Frontierland and Fantasyland on the bridge to see one of the last remnants of Rainbow Ridge and Rainbow Caverns

> Original attractions in Frontierland at the opening of Disneyland included the Rainbow Ridge Pack Mules, Rainbow Caverns Mine Train and the Conestoga Wagon attractions.
>
> The tunnel at the exit of Big Thunder Mountain Railroad and the tunnel you see on the bridge are two of the remnants of these rides. If you watch the water in front of the tunnel you will also see fish jump from time to time. These fish are animatronic fish and never get tired of jumping through the pond.

☐ Ride the Mark Twain Riverboat and explore the Rivers of America in old fashion style

> The Mark Twain Riverboat is an authentic paddleboat taking guests down the Rivers of America. While on board, you will hear your narrator talk about the

attractions on the river front of New Orleans Square and Pirates Lair.

The Mark Twain was very special to Walt Disney as he and his wife Lillian celebrated their wedding anniversary on this very boat just days before Disneyland opened to the public.

☐ Find one of the original keel boats from the Mike Fink Keel Boat attraction on the Rivers of America

This attraction began operation in December 1955 and took guest across the Rivers of America until 1997 when the Gullywhumper tipped over, spilling several guests into the river. While no one was injured, the attraction was closed and this one boat pay homage to this classic Disneyland attraction.

☐ Ride the Sailing Ship Columbia and experience the Rivers of America just like the buccaneers

The Columbia is a replica of the Columbia Rediviva, the first ship to circumnavigate the globe. This eighty-foot tall sailing ship allows guests to ride along the deck or walk through the sailor's quarters during their voyage.

Enjoy a leisurely ride down the river on this classic sailing vessel.

*One hundred things you need to do at Disneyland before you die*

☐ Stop off at the shipping office on the banks of the Rivers of America

Find the mural of the Mark Twain on the side of the shipping office and you may see a very familiar character on the deck.

This quiet mural has graced the banks of the Rivers of America for decades but few know the secret hidden on the deck of the Mark Twain in the picture.

None other than famous Mickey Mouse graces the deck riding along with the other guests floating down the river.

☐ Find the petrified tree in Frontierland

Walt Disney was always looking for something to include in his theme parks and this authentic petrified tree is one of those items.

While rumors suggest Walt purchased this for his wife on their anniversary, the Disney family has long since debunked this rumor and has explain what actually happened when Disney acquired the oldest attraction at Disneyland.

Just three days shy of their wedding anniversary, Walt and Lillian were travelling through Colorado when Walt stopped in at Pikes Petrified Forest attraction while Lillian waited in the car.

When he emerge, he has purchased the fossil you see before you. Always one for a joke, Walt encourage the story of this being Lillian's anniversary gift until the rumor became a legend.

☐ Stop at the Stage Door café for a hot dog or funnel cake

Around the corner from the Golden Horseshoe, you will find the Stage Door café offering guests quick bites along their dusty travels. Cool drinks and hot dogs are on the menu, or for a sweet treat, perhaps ice cream or funnel cake for those with a sweet tooth.

# Adventureland

Get ready to explore the wilds of the jungle when you travel to exotic places and test your limits.

See how Tarzan and Jane live as you climb to the treetops above Disneyland. Travel down the rivers of the world with your Disneyland river guide or dare to enter the Temple of the Forbidden Eye with doctor Indiana Jones.

Whatever speaks to the adventurer in you, you will have a wild time in Adventureland.

☐ Get a Dole Whip at the famed Enchanted Tiki Room

Any day you cross over into the Adventureland area, you will find a long line of people waiting just outside the preshow for The Enchanted Tiki Room. This line is not for an attraction or character, it is for the famous Dole Whip Pineapple soft serve.

While Dole began serving their pineapple juice at Disneyland in the 1960's, Dole Whip has been served at Disneyland since 1986. For those who have never tried this Hawaiian treat, it is an excellent way to cool off on a hot summer day.

☐ Watch a live performance of The Enchanted Tiki Room

The birds and flowers of the Enchanted Tiki Room were some of the first animatronics developed for Disneyland along with Great Moments with Mr. Lincoln and It's a Small World.

The anthem for the Tiki Room, written by the Sherman brothers, also known for writing songs for *Mary Poppins* starring Julie Andrews and *Bed Knobs and Broomsticks* starring Angela Lansbury.

This marked the first time in Disneyland history that a song was written specifically for an attraction. The Tiki Room has remained the same since it premiered in June 1963.

Along with the singing birds and flowers, one of the cast members of the Tiki Room has become just as famous as the attraction itself. Maynard has been working with Disneyland, sometimes here or at The Haunted Mansion but guests love to get a picture with Maynard and have him sign their autograph books.

☐ Get a special treat at the Tropical Hideaway

> The Tropical Hideaway is a newer area in Adventureland offering guests a variety of snacks along their travels.
>
> Enjoy a pineapple raspberry swirl or pineapple orange swirl dole whip. Try the delicious bao with meat or vegetables while enjoying the al fresco dining area.

☐ Find Rosita mentioned in the Enchanted Tiki Room

> If you listen carefully while enjoying the Enchanted Tiki Room, you will here one of your hosts talk about the missing Rosita.
>
> Here at the Tropical Hideaway you can meet her for yourself. Rosita loves to get pictures and talk to the guests during the day.
>
> Be sure to visit with Rosita while at the Tropical Hideaway.

☐ Stop in the shops in Adventureland and get your fortune from Aladdin's Other Lamp

> Hidden in an alcove within the shops of Adventureland, you can hear the lamp give you wisdom for a small fee. The Genie may be a little sassy with you but his wisdom is true. Look closely

or you may just walk right by as this item is hidden from guests in his own alcove at the back of this shop.

☐ Visit Rajah's Mint to get a special penny pressed

There are penny press machines all over Disneyland resort offering different designs stamped into pennies, but at Rajah's Mint, you can hear the stamp of this press like a hammer hitting a nail.

After inserting your coins, stand back and hear the ear-splitting sound of the hammer hitting your penny and creating this life long souvenir of Adventureland and Rajah's Mint.

☐ Get your fortune read by Shrunken Ned, the explorer

Ned is now a permanent fixture in Adventureland and gives his advice for a small fee. Simply place your hand on the platform and deposit your coin and Ned will come to life to speak his wisdom from within his case inside the shops of Adventureland.

Be sure to take the fortune card Ned gifts you before you go as a souvenir of your time with Shrunken Ned.

☐ Ride the Jungle Cruise

> Explore the rivers of the jungle with your expert safari and marvel at the wonders you will see on the rivers of the world.
>
> Travel down the river to the African savannah where you will see animals at the river's edge. Find the lost safari group or watch as the gorilla take over the camp.
>
> Observe a native tribe but be careful you don't get ambushed. Finally, see the eighth wonder of the world before you head back to civilization.

☐ Get a souvenir map of the Jungle Cruise

> Once your cruise through the jungle is done, you don't have to forget where you have been. Ask a skipper for an authentic Jungle Cruise map at the exit. This gift is one of the best kept secrets of Adventureland.

☐ Meet your favorite Adventureland characters

> Aladdin and Jasmine, Moana and even the Genie may be strolling along ready to take pictures and sign your autograph book.

You never know which of your favorite Adventureland characters might turn up at any moment along the jungle paths of Adventureland.

☐ Explore the lost temple with Indiana Jones and the Temple of the Forbidden Eye

Hidden deep in the jungle, the famed Dr. Jones has found this ancient temple and now it is your turn to discover the secrets within. Pack your hat, whip and gun for this adventure that you may never return from.

☐ Find the traps set by the natives as you walk through the queue for Indiana Jones and the Temple of the Forbidden Eye

As you set on the path to discover the gifts of Mara, be careful or you may set of some of the booby traps within the temple. Step on the wrong stone and the roof may collapse on you, pull a suspicious bamboo support or pull the rope that suspends a priceless artifact.

If you can avoid the pitfalls on your way, you will find yourself eye to eye with Mara.

☐ Decode the ancient writing on the walls in the queue for Indiana Jones at the Temple of the Forbidden Eye

As you work your way through the queue, you will see mysterious writing along the walls. These writings are a remnant of the past of this attraction. During the first years of Indiana Jones, guests were handed a special card with a decoder on it to help them translate the writings into English. These cards kept guests busy during the long waits for this attraction.

While the decoder cards are long gone, you can find copies of the code on fan sites throughout the internet so you can decode these ancient writings for yourself.

☐ Find the home of the little man of Disneyland

Just outside the entrance to Indiana Jones, there is a very small house hidden within the trees. Guests walk by every day without ever knowing this tiniest of details exist.

In 1955, the Disney company released a children's book about the little man of Disneyland, a leprechaun who lives in a tree in Anaheim. Mickey, Donald and Goofy come to the property to decide which trees to clear for Disneyland and the little man is very unhappy about this.

The trio take him to Disney studios in a helicopter to show him the blueprints for the new theme park and offer to build him a home in the park. While he refuses them, and disappears to find a new place to live, this little house remains for him if he ever returns.

☐ Walk through Tarzan's Treehouse

Walk up to the treetops above Disneyland to find the home of Tarzan and find where the ape man grew up after Sabor attacked his family.

Find the baby Tarzan with Sabor ready to attack. Continue your exploration of the treehouse and evidence of the inhabitants.

Watch as you touch the images of Tarzan in his book and see his childhood come to life. You can ever see how Jane sketches Tarzan before finishing your time at the camp playing with the instruments left for the next traveler.

☐ Find some friends from the film *Beauty and the Beast* at the camp at the base of Tarzan's Treehouse

As you come down from the tree top, you will enter the camp with many items left behind by the explorers. If you look very closely, you may find two items that look very familiar.

Within the camp, you will find Mrs. Potts and Chip among the items. Be sure to get a picture of these silent friends from another fairy tale story.

☐ Play with the instruments in the camp at Tarzan's Treehouse

Within the camp at the base of Tarzan's Treehouse, you will find many items that have been left behind by the explorers. Be sure to try your hand at banging some of the pots and pans together or make your own music with the bamboo reeds strung together.

Fun can be had for every age in the camp at Tarzan's Treehouse.

Enjoy a hearty kabob at Bengal Barbeque

For guests looking for a yummy kabob, Bengal Barbeque offers a variety of treats. Whether you fancy chicken, beef, pork or vegetables, Bengal Barbeque offers something for every taste.

# New Orleans Square

Meander through the streets and alleys of this water front city to explore the sights and sounds that are only found in New Orleans. Grab a mint julep while listening to the jazz stylings of Jambalaya Jazz or grab some gumbo before your travel through the caves below to find the Pirate of the Caribbean.

Keep a close eye on your valuables for you may come face to face with the redheaded pirate. Finish your time in New Orleans Square with 999 happy haunts on the abandoned mansion left by Master Gracey.

Hungry on your travels? Get a bowl of clam chowder in a sourdough bread bowl and top it off with some yummy beignets.

*One hundred things you need to do at Disneyland before you die*

☐ Stand below Walt Disney's apartment above Pirates of the Caribbean

High above the Pirate of the Caribbean attraction sits a quiet spot very few guests ever get a chance to see. This apartment was built for Walt Disney and his family since the apartment above the fire house on Main Street became too small.

While Disney never lived to make use of it, the apartment has had several uses over the years. For many years, the suite was used as a store which allowed guests to walk through the rooms mean for the Disney family.

With the 50$^{th}$ anniversary of Disneyland, the apartment was once more converted into a suite and very lucky families would be selected to spend the night in this very special place.

Recently, this apartment was transformed once again to create a once in a lifetime dining experience. For the low cost of fifteen thousand dollars, you and nine of your special friends can experience a seven-course dinner complete with wine pairings, cocktails and three butlers to serve your every wish.

Make your reservations today.

☐ Find the initials of the Disney brothers on the balcony of the Disney apartment

The balcony of the Disney suite dons elaborate ironwork but, hidden within, you will find gold initials W.D. and R.D. These are the initials of Walt and Roy Disney. The two brothers were partners throughout their career, Walt the dreamer and Roy the businessman.

These elaborate gold letters are a silent tribute to the Disney family and the apartment that stands within the theme park.

☐ Stop to read the 30th anniversary dedication plaque in the queue for Pirates of the Caribbean

On March 7, 1997 Disneyland rededicated The Pirates of the Caribbean, giving the contributors credit for their work on this attraction.

If you read carefully you will find the words, "The Original" at the top of the plaque meaning this was the first incarnation of Pirates of the Caribbean to be created. In addition, at the bottom it reads, "Yo Ho Yo Ho a pirate's life for me", referring to the famous song sung throughout the attraction.

☐ Ride along with Captain Jack Sparrow, Barbosas, Davy Jones and the pirates of Pirates of the Caribbean

Travel through a quiet New Orleans bayou before plunging down to where the remains of pirates stand silently below the ground.

Be careful if you spy the cursed treasure or you may be sent back to the time of Pirates. Help Captain Barbossa locate Captain Jack Sparrow while pirates loot the city. Can you escape before the city is destroyed?

☐ Find the Captain Jack Sparrow Voo Doo doll in the window of Pieces of Eight

Standing just outside the exit of Pirates of the Caribbean, you will find Pieces of Eight, the shop dedicated to everything Pirates. Most guests walk right past the elaborate window without noticing a small doll resting within the treasure.

Captain Jack Sparrow has been the target of voodoo as his voodoo doll sits waiting for the master to torture the unsuspecting Captain Jack along his adventures.

- [ ] Get your fortune told by Fortune Red in the alley of New Orleans Square

    Hidden in a private alley of New Orleans Square stands Fortune Red waiting for unsuspecting guests to give him a silver coin to tell their fortune.

    Do you trust this marauder to tell you the truth? Give him a quarter and take a chance.

    Make sure you take the souvenir fortune he gives you before you go on your way.

- [ ] Get your portrait done by a New Orleans Square artist

    Tucked away in the alleys of New Orleans Square you will find some of the most talented artist at Disneyland. Sit with one of these portrait artists and let them turn you into your favorite character or create an original design for you.

    Not only talented at portraits, stop to see some of their artwork around this area and marvel at the exquisite talent of these artists.

- [ ] Visit the exclusive Club 33

    While you must be a member or know a member to gain entry, this is a once in a lifetime experience giving guests the opportunity to dine high above New Orleans Square.

Originally planned by Walt Disney to entertain honored guests, Disney never lived to see his dream come true, but Disney imagineers created this experience for guest who can afford the steep price tag.

Whether you dine at Club 33 for a special occasion or just an evening out, this experience is one of the most exclusive at Disneyland.

☐ Listen to the musical style of Jambalaya Jazz.

Take some time out of your busy day to sing along with your favorite Jazz tunes.

The Jambalaya Jazz appear hourly throughout New Orleans Square and perform for visitors throughout the year. As you walk through this area, you will suddenly hear a very familiar tune played live. Stop for a while and you may get a souvenir necklace to wear during your day.

Feel free to make a request or let them play for you on your birthday,

☐ Find the anchor of famed pirate Jean Lafitte

> Down near the Rivers of America you will find a very old anchor sitting quietly among the stairs leading up to the heart of New Orleans Square.
>
> This anchor, an artifact from the ship of Jean Lafitte, was first seen in Frontierland when Disneyland opened and later moved to this spot in New Orleans Square to remind guest of the rich history surrounding New Orleans.

☐ Find the mysterious crypt 1764

> Rumored to be one of the last remnants of an early attraction concept in New Orleans Square, this walled off archway remains a Disney secret. As with most of Disneyland, imagineers created concepts for rides that would never become a reality.
>
> One concept was for a walk-through tunnel system leading from the shores of the Rivers of America to what was then Tom Sawyer Island. This concept would be keeping in the theme of Pirates of the Caribbean but proved to be too complex. The imagineers decided to concentrate their efforts on other attractions so this wall is a remainder of this planned attraction.

☐ Enjoy a warm bowl of soup at Royal Street Veranda or Pacific Wharf Café

A guest favorite while visiting New Orleans Square is a hot bowl of clam chowder or gumbo in a freshly made bread bowl. The ultimate comfort food, these tasty soups offer guests a great meal.

The bread bowls are made daily at Disneyland resort and available to take home at Boudin's Bakery in Disney California Adventure.

☐ Listen for the ghost horse in front of the funeral coach at The Haunted Mansion

Walk through the gate of this bayou mansion to find things aren't at all what they seem to be. In front of this stately manor sits an antique funeral coach waiting to take the next body to the cemetery.

Listen to the distinct whiny of the horse ready to pull the coach even though you cannot see the animal the sound is coming from.

☐ Join the ranks of the ghosts by applying at Ghost Relations

Within the funeral coach outside the Haunted Mansion you will find a help wanted sign. If you read this hilarious sign, you can apply for a permanent position at the Haunted Mansion.

Apply at Ghost Relations please.

☐ Read the epitaphs in the pet cemetery garden in front of the Haunted Mansion

It is not only the humans that have an eternal place at this ancient house. Here lie the beloved pets of the residents immortalized with clever tombstones.

Freddy the bat has a stone that can be read both ways. Note the cat's headstone includes several smaller stones for all of the birds he took with him. Standing in the center of the garden is Buddy the dog, faithful to the end.

Behind the pets in the garden, you will find on the wall some more exotic pets immortalized. Jeb the spider got caught is his own web while the snake caught the gardener by surprise.

☐ Read the epitaphs on the hillside cemetery

High of the hillside behind the Haunted Mansion, you will find several tombstones hidden in the vines and trees.

This small cemetery is not just decoration for the mansion and its inhabitants, it also stands as a memorial to all of the imagineers that put their signature on the Haunted Mansion and Disneyland park.

Included in this cemetery are the names, X Atencio who wrote the Haunted Mansion theme song, Marc Davis, who created many of the special effects and characters, Claude Coats the lead designer of the attraction and Yale Gracey creator of special effects. Gracey is also the namesake of the owner of The Haunted Mansion, Master Gracey.

This little cemetery is not the first time the imagineers have been immortalized at this attraction. The first time, when the attraction opened in 1969 when the stones were place between the queues in the area that is now the garden. Later they were moved to the hillside and were removed when they fell into disrepair. Now these grave markers are back and ready for pictures to immortalize your time at the Haunted Mansion.

☐ Look for the bird house dressed in Haunted Mansion fashion to match the house

Another new addition to the Haunted Mansion is a small birdhouse on the far side of the house near the hillside cemetery. While you may not have the opportunity to see the birdhouse on a day where the wait time is short, on busier days you will find this hidden little gem.

☐ Ride in a doom buggy to visit The Haunted Mansion

The Haunted Mansion attraction opened at Disneyland in August 1969 but the concept for the ghostly attraction had very different beginnings.

Originally, designs for this attraction included a walk-through museum of oddities and a boat ride through a sunken mansion. Finally, in 1969, the attraction you see opened to the public with the famous Doom Buggies.

While this attraction has remained mostly the same since opening day, there have been some changes. During the 1980's, a live actor would scare guests by lunging at the ride vehicles. More recently is the addition of the Hat Box Ghost, a character only reference by maintenance notes from the 1970's. The ghost is now a permanent part of this beloved attraction.

Now you can brave the great beyond at the Haunted Mansion.

☐ Travel across the Rivers of America to Pirates Lair

At the shore of the Rivers of America you will find a small dock with a raft waiting to take guest across the river to play at Pirates Lair. This attraction has been a working part of Disneyland since the early years.

This short trip is reminiscent of the raft Huckleberry Finn took in the famous book by Mark Twain. The island, once named Tom Sawyer Island, has since been taken over by pirates and turn into the Pirates Lair.

☐ Dare to enter the pirate caves and discover the pirates living and haunting the islands caves

As your raft lands on Pirates Lair and you begin your exploration of the island, you will come across a cave entrance with a warning from Captain Jack Sparrow himself. Do you dare dismiss this warning and enter the cave?

Should you choose to enter, you may just find a treasure or something more. Inside this dark cave, listen for the heart of Davy Jones, check out the jail cell built into this cavern or reach for some real pirate booty. Be careful that things may not appear until the light of the full moon shows them for what they really are.

☐ Find the pirates treasure on Pirates Lair

Somewhere during your exploration of Pirates Lair you may stumble upon a treasure so large no chest will hold it.

Should you find this treasure and the pirates flag flying behind it, feel free to get some fun pictures behind or even on top of this vast treasure.

☐ Climb through the caverns and pirates ship

Throughout Pirates Lair you will find a honeycomb of caverns to climb through. When you enter the ship's hull, listen for strange noises and pirate artifacts left behind.

This labyrinth of caves is ripe for exploring so be sure to spend some time amongst the caves at Pirates Lair.

☐ Play in the ship wreck and bone cage

At the edge of the waterways on Pirates Lair, you will come across a pirate ship wrecked and half sunken. Play among the ruins of this pirate vessel by turning the cranks or draining the water to see what is revealed. The skeletal pirates still cling to their treasure from beyond the grave may be just one of the strange items you come across.

Do not miss an opportunity to get a picture in the iconic bone cage from the second installment of the *Pirates of the Caribbean* films before continuing your exploration of the island.

☐ Visit the blacksmith shop where Will Turner worked in *Pirates of the Caribbean*

Near the front of Pirates Lair you will find a shop with a sign that reads, "Blacksmith, Ships hardware, Swords, Chains forged and repaired." Read the name just above and you will see W. Turner Prop.

Step inside and you will find swords lying about, waiting for their new owners. This small blacksmith shop is owned by Will Turner who helped Captain Jack Sparrow in the *Pirates of the Caribbean* films.

☐ Ride the Disneyland railroad from New Orleans Square

The Disneyland railroad makes a complete circle of the theme park and stops in various area of the park. For your convenience while in New Orleans Square, hope aboard the train to travel in comfort to your next destination in the park.

☐ Listen to the opening day speech in Morse code

Guests arriving on the platform to wait for the train will see a railroad office on the opposite side of the track but most do not notice the subtle sound of the telegraph tapping out a message in Morse code.

This tapping or clicking sound is sending Walt Disney's opening day speech through the telegraph wire throughout the day. This is just another example of the attention to detail Disneyland offers guests throughout the theme park.

☐ Enjoy Beignets at the French Quarter

Tucked away in a corner of New Orleans Square is a treat guests line up for every day. Mickey shaped Beignets are a treat for the sight as well as the taste.

These lightly fried doughnuts are covered in powered sugar and guests get them hot from the fryer to enjoy. Be sure to get your tasty treat throughout the year as the flavor of these beignets change with the seasons. Guests can sometimes find pumpkin spice or peppermint beignets during the holiday seasons so be sure to go back regularly to find a new favorite.

☐ Have a meal at the French Quarter

The French Quarter restaurant makes authentic New Orleans cuisine to tempt guests when they get hungry. Be sure to try the gumbo or a Po Boy sandwich in this al fresco dining experience.

Enjoy the strains of the Jambalaya Jazz playing for guests at various time during the day to complete the New Orleans experience.

☐ Enjoy dining at the Blue Bayou

> The Blue Bayou restaurant, resting on the shore of the Pirates of the Caribbean attraction, offers guests a high-class dining experience in a bayou setting.
>
> Sip a cool beverage and enjoy a sumptuous meal while watching the boats of the Pirates of the Caribbean floating by.
>
> Do not miss this one of a kind dining experience.

☐ Visit the Mlle Antoinette's Parfumerie at New Orleans Square

> Along the alleyways of New Orleans Square, you will find Mlle Antoinette's Parfumerie. Inside you will find all of your favorite scents or an exciting new perfume. Be sure to ask for assistance from the experts to help you find the scent that will work with your body chemistry to accentuate your natural beauty.

☐ Visit the Cristal D'Orleans shop

> One of the loveliest shops in New Orleans Square is the Cristal D'Orleans Shop. Inside, you will find everything from hand blown figures, etched crystal goblets and crystal tiaras. The choices are limitless when you enter the Cristal D'Orleans Shop.

Find your new favorite souvenir today at the Cristal D'Orleans Shop.

☐ Get a Disney themed dapper day outfit at Le Bat en Rouge

While Dapper Day is an unofficial yearly event at Disneyland, the flavor of this event can be found within Le Bat en Rouge. From dresses to petticoats to purses and fasteners, you will find your favorite characters and themes within this shop in New Orleans Square.

☐ Dress like your favorite pirate at Pieces of Eight

Pieces of Eight offers guests a wide variety of apparel to choose from along with accessories and toys for everyone in your party.

Get your new buccaneer hat or T shirt to show your pirate side. Pirates costumes for the little ones or toy sets will be the perfect item to take home giving you great memories of your time in New Orleans Square.

☐ Find Haunted Mansion treasures in Port Royal Curios and Curiosities

For those looking for a wide variety of Haunted Mansion or Nightmare Before Christmas themed merchandise, stop at the Port Royal Curios and Curiosities shop on Royal Street.

Whether it is a new T shirt or decorations for your home, this store has everything you can imagine to bring the Haunted Mansion home with you.

☐ Dine at Café Orleans

Whether it is Breakfast or Lunch, Café Orleans offers guests delicious food while dining al fresco.

Enjoy the sites and sound of Disneyland while you enjoy a great meal.

# Critter Country

Enter a place where the animals are leading the fun and happiness is king. Towering above this small part of Disneyland is Splash Mountain where every day is a happy day.

Visit the candy shop where you can watch the candy makers creating todays treats. Fly down a fifty-foot flume after visiting the gang from *Song of the South*.

Join Winnie the Pooh in the Hundred Acre Wood with all of Christopher Robins friends to relive the *Many Adventures of Winnie the Pooh* starring you in the middle of the fun.

- [ ] Travel down the Rivers of America on the Davy Crockett Explorer Canoes

    One of the lesser known of the Disneyland attractions can be found in Critter Country at the banks of the Rivers of America. Travel in an old fashion canoe on a complete circle around Pirates Lair Island just like the early explorers like Lewis and Clark or Davey Crockett.

This is an incredible way to explore the river and see the treasure hidden around the river bend but keep in mind, the guests propel these vessels so get your arms ready for a workout.

☐ Find the carrots growing through the roof of the Briar Batch

The first shop you come across on your path through Critter Country is The Briar Patch shop. This little shop hides a big secret as you look at the roof to see giant carrots coming through. Just one of these carrots could feed a rabbit family.

Look around The Briar Patch and you will find portraits of the famous residents of Splash Mountain, Brer Rabbit and Brer Fox.

Be sure to pick up your new mouse ears before you leave this charming little shop.

☐ Find the restrooms commemorating the Country Bear Jamboree

One of the first attraction seen in this area of Disneyland was the classic Country Bear Jamboree. While this attraction has been retired for quite some time, the performers remain in small ways. One such way are the pictures above the doorway at the bathrooms at the Hungry Bear Restaurant.

You will find the portrait of Gomer, the piano player for the country bears, outside the men's room and Trixie's portrait above the lady's powder room. For those who remember with fondness the country bears, this is a small reminder of a joyful memory.

☐ Enjoy a hearty meal at the Hungry Bear restaurant

Whether it is burgers, French fries, salads or vegan specialties, the Hungry Bear in Critter Country offers guests a great meal with spectacular views of the Rivers of America and the mountains of Batuu.

Enjoy these great food choices in an al fresco setting in this rustic area of Disneyland.

☐ Fall down a fifty-foot plunge of Splash Mountain and visit the characters from the Walt Disney classic *Song of the South*

Another mountain peak to grace the mountain range of Disneyland is Splash Mountain. Walk through the old barn to board a hollow log and explore the wilderness that makes up this enchanted mountain.

Along your way you will find some friends from the Disney classic *Song of the South*. Br'er Fox and

Br'er Bear are trying to catch Br'er Rabbit for their supper. Hopefully you can help this little rabbit from getting caught.

Find Mr. Blue Bird and sing along to a classic Disney tune before climbing the peak to Br'er Foxes lair. Hold on when you fall fifty feet into the briar patch below to escape with your life.

Finish your time at Splash Mountain by celebrating with the gang from America Sings. This now retired attraction took guests on a trip through musical history and the animated singers and dancers were brought to entertain a whole new generation of guests on Splash Mountain.

☐ Visit the hundred-acre wood with The Many Adventures of Winnie the Pooh

Travel through the pages of your favorite stories to see Winnie the Pooh, Tigger, Piglet, Eeyore and Rabbit in the adventures you have known since childhood.

Get swept away in the flood from the rain storm, get blown away on a blustery day and fight Heffalump's and Woozles to keep Pooh's honey safe.

Join in to celebrate Pooh's birthday before your time with Winnie the Pooh ends.

- [ ] Find the heads of Max, Buff, and Melvin within The Many Adventures of Winnie the Pooh

    Previously houses in the space that is now The Many Adventures of Winnie the Pooh was The Country Bear Jamboree attraction. While the bears have retired from performing for guests, there is one part of the show that still remains.

    The three heads mounted on the wall of the Country Bear Theaters were Buff the buffalo, Max the deer and Melvin the moose. If you look above you when exiting the Heffalump and Woozle room, you will see these three silently watching you from above.

- [ ] Stop in a Pooh Corner and taste some delicious sweet treats

    At the end of Critter Country, you will find one of the sweetest shops in Disneyland.

    Pooh Corner houses a candy store to temp your sweet tooth. Try a Tigger Tail or gourmet candy apple made fresh every day. Watch as the candy makers create cake pops decorated as your favorite characters.

    If candy is more your taste, get a bag of your favorite sweets to keep you going.

☐ Find the house of Mr. Bluebird in Critter Country

> Just outside Pooh corner you will find a small house for the special little resident of Critter Country, Mr. Blue Bird. As the song says, Mr. Blue Birds on your shoulder. Here you get to see where he lives at the base of Splash Mountain.

☐ Visit Winnie the Pooh and his friends

> Throughout the day in Critter Country you can meet your favorite friends from the stories of Winnie the Pooh. Pooh, Eeyore, Tigger and Piglet visit with guests to take pictures and sign autographs for some wonderful memories.
>
> Be sure to stop by for fun with the friends of Critter Country.

☐ Find the homes of the characters from Winnie the Pooh

> The homes of Rabbit, Eeyore and Piglet can be found on the small river in front of the Many Adventures of Winnie the Pooh attraction in Critter Country. These small houses can be seen decorated for the Christmas holiday if your visiting during the holiday season.

# Tomorrowland

Get ready to rocket into the future as you explore the furthest reaches of space at Tomorrowland.

When Disneyland opened in 1955, Tomorrowland represented the year 1986 with flying saucers and rocket packs showing guests what they could expect thirty years in the future. These days, Tomorrowland is more about the future as seen in your favorite movies.

Fly with Star Tours to make sure you get the rebel spy transported to the base, Ride through space on Space Mountain or ride along with Buzz Lightyear to save the galaxy from the evil emperor Zurg.

Ride in your own car along the quiet roads of Autopia and finally and visit with your favorite Star Wars characters at Launch Bay.

*One hundred things you need to do at Disneyland before you die*

☐ Ride through space on the Astro Orbitor

Ride through the air in your own rocket ship on the Astro Orbitor. Framing the entrance to Tomorrowland, the Astro Orbitor offers guests of all ages a fun ride with spectacular views of Tomorrowland and the Hub or Disneyland.

Do not miss this blast off in Tomorrowland.

☐ Visit Star Tours and save the rebel spy from Darth Vader

Get ready to board a space cruiser and take off to travel through space but keep on the lookout for Darth Vader as he hunts for a rebel spy.

Jump through hyperspace to race through the ice of Hoth, the forest of Kashyyk or Tatooine to escape capture.

☐ Save the galaxy from the evil Emperor Zurg on Buzz Lightyear Astro Blasters

Join Buzz Lightyear to save the galaxy from the evil Emperor Zurg as you enter your space vehicle to shoot the targets and recover the battery cells.

This adorable attraction, based on the Toy Story films, offers guests an interactive experience to shoot at targets and gain points. When your ride comes to an end, check your score and see what space ranger level you have achieved.

Be sure to email your picture to your personal account to keep a great souvenir of your time with Buzz Lightyear.

☐ Find the perfect souvenir at Little Green Men Store Command

Little Green Men Store Command offers guests a wide variety of souvenirs from your favorite Pixar films.

Find a soft plush or a Buzz Lightyear figure for your collection. A variety of pins for the trader or toys that will be the perfect reminder of your day in Tomorrowland.

☐ Find a great Star Wars gift at The Star Trader

Make your fantasy of becoming a real Jedi a reality at the Star Trader in Tomorrowland. Among the amazing Star Wars collectibles, you can dress like your favorite Star Wars characters.

Pick from dozens of options to find the perfect Star Wars themed gift to take home and fantasize about being a Jedi.

*One hundred things you need to do at Disneyland before you die*

☐ Fly through the galaxy on Hyperspace Mountain

Join the battle in space as you board a space ship and take off through Hyperspace Mountain.

Space Mountain was created in 1977, one of the last attractions Walt Disney assisted in designing. For decades, Space Mountain has been thrilling guests. At times, Space Mountain has been updated to include rock and roll music and lights but the latest incarnation includes the thrill of Star Wars Star Destroyers and X Wing Fighters to bring guest a whole new experience.

☐ Watch extended first run movie previews in Tomorrowland

Near the entrance to Space Mountain, guests can sit back and watch extended previews of the newest films coming to a theater near you. Whether it is a Pixar films or the latest Disney Animation film, you will not want to miss this golden opportunity to see these film clips first.

☐ Grab a slice of pizza or pasta at Pizza Planet

For those hungry during their travels in Tomorrowland, stop at Pizza Planet for a slice of your favorite pizza or tempting pasta dishes. This Pixar themed restaurant displays fun posters of your favorite Toy Story characters to enjoy while dining.

☐ Drive your own car on the roads of Autopia

> Jump in your car and race around the track at Autopia. One of the original attraction on opening day in 1955, Autopia had no raised center track allowing guests to drive off the road at times.
>
> Over the years, the track has been revised and the cars updated but this great ride still creates smiles for guests.

☐ Get your driver's license made at Autopia

> Get the ultimate souvenir of your ride on Autopia. At the exit you will find a small booth to create this one of a kind souvenir. For a small fee you can get your picture taken on an authentic Disneyland driver's license.
>
> Smile for the picture and take home a great souvenir for your wallet.

☐ Travel under the ocean to visit with Nemo and his friends on the Finding Nemo Submarine Voyage

> The submarines you are about to board came to Disneyland in 1959 to recreate the world of the Nautilus from *20,000 Leagues Under the Sea*. The submarine voyage took guests along ancient ruins and into the darkness of the ocean to see sea creatures real and mythical.

The submarines were retired for many years, leaving the lagoon empty but still a lovely place to take pictures.

In 2007, Disneyland reopened the submarines with a new Finding Nemo theme and guests flocked to the attraction once more.

☐ Get your selfie with the seagulls from *Finding Nemo*

The Finding Nemo submarine lagoon is a stunning picture spot for people looking for a souvenir picture but, for those looking for a fun selfie, be sure to get a picture with the seagulls sitting atop the buoy.

These "Mine mine mine" seagulls are still looking for their snack but you can capture them in your pictures before they fly away.

☐ Find the spot where three different fences come together

In a quiet corner of Disneyland, guest can follow the fence from the Finding Nemo lagoon to a corner near the roadway of Autopia. In this corner, three different decorative fences come together but are rarely noticed by the guests strolling by on the walkways.

For those looking for an obscure detail, be sure to hunt down this random area straddling Tomorrowland and Fantasyland.

☐ Enjoy a quick bite at Tomorrowland Terrace

Looking for something quick to restore your energy around Tomorrowland? Stop in at Tomorrowland Terrace and get yourself a burger, salad or a variety of tasty treats in this outdoor setting.

Visit for specialty musical acts or other performances throughout the year. Tomorrowland Terrace has something for every guest.

# Holidays at Disneyland

There is no better time at Disneyland than the holidays. Spend some time peeking the windows on Main Street to see how the creative decorators have carved Jack O' Lanterns. Ride with Jack Skellington and the gang from *The Nightmare Before Christmas* or join the residents of Radiator Springs to see how they have decked out the streets for Halloween.

Christmas brings out the child in every guest who visits and see the amazing Christmas tree and garland throughout Main Street.

Watch the magic of the Christmas lights on Sleeping Beauty Castle or watch spectacular holiday fireworks before it snows on Main Street U.S.A.

Whatever your favorite time of year, you will have a magical time at Disneyland.

# Halloweentime

Join Mickey and all of his friends at the scariest time of year at Disneyland. Whether it is rides, food or characters, you will be immersed in the Halloween fun when you walk through the gates.

See the scariest villains walking the streets and come face to face with these dastardly bad guys and gals.

Get your favorite Disney themed costume together and join in the fun at Mickey's Not So Scary Halloween Party to complete the fun at Disneyland.

☐ Get your picture with the large Mickey pumpkin on Main Street

> Be amazed by the enormous Jack O' Lantern of Mickey Mouse winking at you. Don't miss this great opportunity to get a picture in front of this Halloween icon.

Use your own camera or use PhotoPass to see a little extra holiday magic in your photos.

☐ Get pictures with your favorite characters in their Halloween costumes

Join Mickey, Minnie, Donald, Daisy, Goofy and Pluto as they don their favorite Halloween costumes and pose for pictures throughout the day.

Mickey Mouse as the Vampire, Minnie as a witch, Goofy likes to be a skeleton and Pluto loves his bat collar. Join in the fun of Halloween along with the great characters you love.

☐ Check out the Jack O' Lanterns throughout Main Street U.S.A.

Hidden throughout Main Street you will find hundreds of Jack O'lanterns looking down at you from windows, shop signs and peeking from the windows.

Find the Abraham Lincoln pumpkin, the Dapper Dan's, the shaving pumpkin, the trumpet playing pumpkin and the musical notes pumpkin. The pumpkins above the Mad Hatter shop love to show off their hat collection and top your tour with the Jack O' lanterns at the hub surrounding the Partners statue.

☐ Find the book from Hocus Pocus

> Hidden in the windows of Main Street you may find the iconic book that held Winifred Sanderson's most diabolical spells in the Disney classic *Hocus Pocus*.
>
> This book bound in human skin can be found near Star Bucks coffee house so keep a close eye on the windows.

☐ Get a special Halloween treat at Disneyland

> Throughout the holidays at Disneyland resort the chefs are hard at work creating desserts to get you in the mood for Halloween. Try a mummy macaroon at Jolly Holiday Bakery, stop at the French Market restaurant for a Nightmare Before Christmas inspired cake or taste a heavenly beignet.

☐ Ride Haunted Mansion Holiday

> Take a peek at how Jack Skellington and his friends have transformed the Haunted Mansion for Halloween.
>
> See for yourself Jack's coffin sleigh on the roof with his calculations about Christmas hanging down for you to read. Be amazed by the beautiful stained-glass ornaments before they're shattered. Finally step into your doom buggy to ride through the mansion to see Jack's little ghost dog Zero, the man-eating

wreath, the handmade gingerbread house and finally, the snow-covered graveyard.

To conclude your ride, watch as Oogie Boogie spins his wheel to see what your fate will be before you find your way back to the land of the living.

☐ Get your picture with Jack Skellington and Sally

Join this famous couple from *The Nightmare Before Christmas* while they are visiting New Orleans Square from Halloweentown.

Jack and Sally visit with guests separately and sometimes together throughout the Halloween season so get in line to take pictures and get autographs from this famous duo.

☐ Get a Halloween themed popcorn bucket

Each year, the popcorn carts feature Halloween themed buckets with screen prints of your favorite villains or Halloween characters. For those looking for a truly unique souvenir, you can look forward to character shaped buckets with one of a kind designs.

Be sure to get this treat this Halloween.

☐ Attend the Mickey's Not So Scary Halloween party

> Attending Mickey's No So Scary Halloween Party will be the highlight of your Halloween as you put on your costume and join other Disney fans for this enchanting event.
>
> See Halloween as only Disney can do it, ride your favorite attractions in the darkness, taste the treats and listen to the Cadaver Dan's perform your favorite spooky tunes. The special ticket event offers guests the chance to see Disneyland in a whole new way while the park is attendance is limited so be sure to get your tickets for this yearly event.

☐ Watch the Headless Horseman come down Mainstreet U.S.A.

> Be sure to get your spot for the Halloween parade that makes its way through the park with a very special Halloween character leading the gang.
>
> The headless horseman on his horse will travel the streets of Disneyland with his Jack O' Lantern for all to see. Look for Ichabod Crane cowering somewhere nearby as they head the parade.

☐ Join the fun at the Halloween parade at Mickey's Not So Scary Halloween

Mickey and Minnie lead the fun on this Halloween themed parade only seen during the Mickey's Not so Scary Halloween event.

Your favorite spooky characters dance and sing through the park. Wave to Jack Skellington and Sally with all of their friends. The ballroom dancers from the Haunted Mansion entertain along with the Hitchhiking ghosts and, finally, all of your favorite villains as they celebrate all things Halloween.

☐ Trick or Treat through Disneyland at Mickey's Not So Scary Halloween party

Get your extra-large trick or treat bag out and walk through Disneyland to trick or treat just like when you were a kid.

At locations all over the park, you will find Halloween helpers passing out your favorite treats. Looking for something a little more healthy? Good news, the helpers love to pass out apples and carrots for you to enjoy along with popcorn and crackers.

☐ Find the Halloween tree in Frontierland

An overlooked special tree in Frontierland can be found in front of the Pioneer Mercantile shops.

The Halloween Tree, a 1972 novel by author Ray Bradbury, chronicles the adventures of a group of trick or treaters as they travel through time to save their friend. Throughout their adventures, they learn the origins of Halloween and the traditions we all celebrate today.

The tree you find holds dozens of tiny pumpkins on its branches and a plaque beneath commemorates the night in 2007 when Disneyland brought this tree to life.

☐ Enjoy the Día de los Muertos decorations in Frontierland

In the area around Rancho Del Zocalo, guests will find the Día de los Muertos altars and large figures celebrating the loved ones who have passed on.

Be sure to get pictures with these stunning figures during the Halloweentime events at Disneyland.

# Christmastime at Disneyland

There is no other place on earth happier than Disneyland but add Christmas and all your Christmas wishes have come true. Disneyland and Disney California Adventure are all decked out for the holidays with everything from spectacular Christmas trees, garlands, window displays and holiday themed rides to bring out the childlike wonder in everyone.

Taste your favorite flavors of the holiday or ride your favorite attractions with a Christmas twist, you will have the time of your life during Christmastime.

☐ Witness the splendor of the Disneyland Christmas tree

> The centerpiece to Christmas at Disneyland is the tree on Main Street U.S.A. This sixty-foot-tall tree has over eighteen hundred ornaments and seventy thousand lights. Each evening the cast members

count down to the lighting which makes this tree sparkle like a diamond.

Be sure to get your Christmas photo in front of this Disneyland icon for Christmas.

☐ Listen to the carolers on Main Street

Throughout the Christmas season, you will hear carolers decked out in traditional Christmas costumes, strolling through Main Street shops to serenade guests with your favorite Christmas songs.

If it is your birthday or you just have a request, these talents singers are more than happy to sing your favorite Christmas carol.

☐ Ride Haunted Mansion Holiday

Join Jack Skellington, Sally, Zero and Oogie Boogie and see how they wrecked the halls of the Haunted Mansion with the black garland, the floating Christmas tree made from books, the attic of presents and the giant snake or the cemetery covered in snow.

Find Santa Jack and his companion Zero, Sally gazing at Jack and Oogie Boogie hidden around every turn as an ornament or a cymbal playing toy.

> Don't miss Scary Teddy throughout your ride and watch Oogie Boogie spin the wheel to give you a spooky Christmas surprise.

☐ Experience the Christmas decorations at Disneyland

> Throughout Disneyland resort, the decorators have been hard at work giving every inch of the theme parks the Christmas touch.
>
> Whether it is the wreaths and garland strung across Main Street, the icicle lights dripping off Sleeping Beauty Castle or the traditional masks and feathers in New Orleans Square, you will not want to miss the Christmas decoration throughout the theme parks.
>
> Frontierland boasts corn husk garland and twinkling lights, while residents of Critter Country have put a woodland twist on the holidays with pine cones and fir tree boughs.
>
> Whatever speaks to the child in you, the décor will bring happiness to every guest at Disneyland resort this Christmas season.

☐ Ride It's a Small World Holiday

> The children of the world decorate It's a Small World for Christmas and want to show guests how each country differs

Piñatas for the children of Mexico hold small gifts and candy, dried fruit, nuts and husks decorate the African village, and the children of England decorate with shiny ornaments and garlands.

No matter your favorite country, you will love the holiday spirit of It's a Small World Holiday.

☐ Visit the residents of Toontown and see their zany Christmas décor

Just like everything in Toontown, the holiday décor is as topsy turvy as the characters who have done the decorating.

Visit the gazebo and get a snapshot of the Christmas tree. Visit the various houses and see the décor. Stop at the Toontown fire department and get a picture in the decorated fire engine or visit the gag factory and see their hilarious garlands.

Your holiday visit will not be complete without spending some time in Toontown.

☐ Attend a Candlelight Processional at Disneyland

Listen to the songs of the holidays along with hundreds of Disneyland cast members as they perform for you this Christmas season. See your favorite actors and actresses narrate this spectacular event with holiday themed readings to bring joy to the guests at Disneyland.

You won't want to miss a single moment of the Candlelight Processional.

- [ ] Watch the Disneyland Christmas fireworks

    Each night, Disneyland lights up the sky with the most elaborate way to celebrate the Christmas season.

    Believe in Holiday Magic is an experience you will not want to miss on your visit to Disneyland. With original music created for this show, the fireworks sync up perfectly to bring holiday magic to Disneyland.

- [ ] Experience snow on Main Street

    Top off your visit to Disneyland during the Christmas holiday by experiencing a snow fall on Main Street U.S.A. or at It's a Small World Holiday. Each evening after the fireworks, the imagineers make it snow on the guests in this very special moment.

# Disney California Adventure

# Introduction

Disney California Adventure, opening in February, 2001, created for guests a complete vision of the California landscape from the mountains, oceans, cities and wineries. Attractions inspired by the California landscape brought the entire state to guests visiting one of the newer theme parks in the Disney family.

Originally including an enormous CALIFORNIA sign, original artwork depicting the wonders of California and the Golden Gate bridge in San Francisco. Now visitors experience Buena Vista Street, the California of the 1930's when Walt Disney arrived with his cardboard suitcase and a dream.

Through the years, Disney California Adventure has expanded to include the best of Disney's Pixar films including Car Land and Pixar Pier. Now the excitement of Marvel comes to Disney California Adventure with your favorite super heroes and the all new Guardians of the Galaxy: Mission Breakout.

*Catherine F. Olen*

Today, you can experience the best of your favorite Disney and Pixar films while taking a journey through the marvels of California at Disney California Adventure.

# Buena Vista Street

Go back in time as you stroll down Buena Vista Street of Los Angeles in the 1930's. Visit with the residents, do some shopping or grab a snack as you wander down this charming street.

When your feet get tired, ride the red car to your destination to parts unknown beyond Buena Vista Street.

☐ Visit with the citizens of Buena Vista Street

Along Buena Vista Street, you just may encounter the residents that live in this bustling town. Look out for Milly or Molly on their bicycle, delivering packages. You may find officer Calvin Blue during his rounds to keep the citizens of Buena Vista Street safe. Stop to chat with Donna and she may let you pet her pooch.

The fun continues with your favorite Disney characters Mickey, Minnie, Donald, Daisy, Goofy and Pluto showing off their snappy 1930's clothing while they pose for pictures and sign autographs.

☐ Ride on the Red Car down Buena Vista Street

Why walk when you can ride the shiny Red Car down Buena Vista Street? Ride in comfort as your driver navigates the bustling streets through Buena Vista and Hollywood taking guests to their destination in style.

☐ Find the mail boxes of famous Disney film characters living on Buena Vista Street

Hidden at the top of a short flight of steps on Buena Vista Street are the mail boxes of some of Disney's famous characters.

Included are the mail boxes for Eddie Valiant, the private detective from *Who Framed Roger Rabbit* and Theodore Ogilvie from *The Apple Dumpling Gang*. Be sure to stop by this address of the famous residents of Buena Vista Street.

☐ Visit Julius Katz and Son, be sure to notice the tags on the household appliances waiting for repairs

All along the shelves in Julius Katz and Sons, you will see appliances waiting for the repairman to fix them up good as new. Scatters through the tags describing what need to be repaired, you will find some very strange descriptions. If you read closely on the blue pot you will see "I'm a little teapot…" A small blue clock reads, "Blue, Really?" Far off in a corner is a desk lamp with a tag that reads simply, "Ugly", the poor little lamp.

☐ Visit the windows of Trolley Treats

While the sweets inside tempt guests to rush through the doors of Trolley Treats, stop for a moment to enjoy the whimsical train travelling around the cake mountain with lollypop trees and a chocolate waterfall.

The windows boast miniature train accessories and selections of treats from various eras. Do not miss your chance to see the adorable window displays at Trolley Treats.

☐ Visit Trolley Treats and indulge in some homemade confections

At the end of Buena Vista Street, do not miss an opportunity to step into Trolley Treats to see what the talented confectioners have whipped up for you today.

Fancy a cake pop, a cupcake or even a designer candy apple, they are all here at Trolley Treats.

For those who enjoy the décor, look around the shelves and the top of the room. You will find trains and accessories. Be sure to peek in the window to see the vintage train collections.

☐ Visit Oswald's

Just inside the gates of Disney California Adventure you will find a service station dedicated to one of Walt Disney's first characters, Oswald the Lucky Rabbit. Be sure to stop in and find Oswald merchandise, as well as mouse ears and souvenirs for every guest.

☐ Visit the Los Feliz Five and Dime on Buena Vista Street

This quaint shop reminiscent of the five and dime stores popular in the early days of the twentieth century offers guests a wide variety of souvenirs, mouse ears and toys for guests visiting Disney California Adventure.

If you look at the shelves above, you will see vintage merchandise that was popular during the years when five and dime stores were in every community.

Do not miss this delightful shop on Buena Vista Street.

*One hundred things you need to do at Disneyland before you die*

☐ Visit Big Top Toys

> Beneath the big top, you will find toys for young and old. Everything from cuddly plush characters to play sets from your favorite Disney films will be found in Big Top Toys.
>
> This charming circus themed store is just another example of the attention to detail that Disney offers guests. Do not miss a chance to see Big Top Toys for yourself.

☐ Visit Clarabelle's Hand Scooped ice cream for an ice-cold treat

> Nothing is better on a warm day that hand scooped ice cream from Clarabelle's Ice Cream. In the mood for an ice cream bar? Choose from your favorite flavors and toppings.
>
> For those looking for something hearty, get the kitchen sink sundae with a collectible Mickey or Minnie Mouse sink to take with you as a souvenir.

☐ Find the Dreamers statue of Walt Disney and Mickey Mouse

> Silently watching the guests travel through Buena Vista Street is the Dreamers statue of Walt Disney and his creation Mickey Mouse.

Walt, with his cardboard suitcase, trunk and jacket slung over his shoulder is the picture of what this iconic man looked like when he arrived in Los Angeles. Mickey is the pie-eyed classic character that was voiced by none other than his creator. Be sure to get a picture with this famous duo.

Oh, before you leave take a peek at the bottom of Walt's shoe for a cute surprise.

☐ Have cocktails and appetizers at Carthay Circle lounge

Towering high above Disney California Adventure is the Carthay Circle restaurant. This building is modeled after the Carthay Circle Theater in Los Angeles where *Snow White and the Seven Dwarfs* premiered on December 21, 1937.

When you enter Carthay Circle, you will be met with notices from the premier of *Snow White and the Seven Dwarfs* mounted on the wall of the lobby. Find the window in the lounge where artifacts from the Disney archives are displayed. These treasures are rotated consistently throughout the year so each time you enter this area, you will see something different.

Be sure to have cocktails and snacks in the bar or, for an amazing meal, make reservations for lunch or dinner at Carthay Circle Restaurant.

☐ Watch 5 and Dime perform hits from the 1930's

> Driving through the streets of Hollywood and stopping in front of Carthay Circle you can listen to the song stylings of Five and Dime.
>
> Listen to your favorite songs from the early days of Hollywood from a five-piece band with their front woman, Dime. So, get on your dancing shoes and meet them at the hub by Carthay Circle Restaurant.

☐ Visit Elias and Co. for the latest in Disney clothing

> Find the latest styles for the 1930's in Elias and Company. In addition to the full array of formal clothing being displayed on the mannequins on the second floor, you will also a fine selection of souvenir clothing for your every need.
>
> Whether you are looking for themed T shirts, spirit jerseys or fancy Dapper Day attire, Elias and Company has something new for your closet.

# Hollywood Land

Walk through classic Hollywood and you just might see your favorite celebrity signing autographs along the way.

Stop to see your favorite musical at the Hyperion Theater or watch talented young people performing.

☐ Join the dance party at Disney Junior

> Join your best pal Mickey Mouse and the Disney Junior DJ for an all music, all dancing party starring all your favorite Disney Junior characters.
>
> Sophie the First joins the fun along with Doc McStuffins. See the gang from The Lion Guard via satellite from their home in the pride lands.
>
> Get your dancing shoe on for this fun filled time with your friends from Disney Junior.

☐ Visit Animation Academy to draw your own cartoon

> The Animation Academy is an experience that cannot be missed for the whole family.
>
> Enter this vast space to see your favorite Disney movies playing in 360 vision around you.
>
> Tucked away in the secret part of the Animation Academy find the chamber where you create your own animated cartoon to take with you as a souvenir or take the quiz in the beast's library to find out which character you would be.

☐ Get your picture with Princess Anna and Queen Elsa at the Frozen meet and greet

> The royalty of Arendelle have arrived at Disney California Adventure and now you can meet Princess Anna and Queen Elsa.
>
> Stop by for pictures and autographs from these royal sisters during your time at the Animation Academy.

☐ Take the drawing class at Animation Academy

> Find out what it feels like to be a Disney animator. Join the talented artists as they show you, step by step, how to draw your favorite characters.

Be sure to check the board outside the Animation Academy to see at which hour the character of your dreams is being drawn.

☐ Have a chat with Crush the turtle in Turtle Talk

Join Crush at the human viewing screen to chat with your favorite turtle from the E.A.C.

Learn to talk turtle and ask Crush your questions as he answers all the questions you have always wanted to know about him and his friends. Keep an eye out for some of his friend who stop by to visit from time to time.

☐ See Mickey's PhilharMagic

Join Mickey Mouse as he gets ready for the concert. Beware as Donald Duck tries his hand at being the conductor when he dons Mickey's sorcerer's hat and mayhem commences.

Join your favorite songs as Donald jumps into the movie that have made Disney famous.

☐ Travel with Mike and Sulley to save Boo from Randall in Monster's Inc. Mike and Sulley to the Rescue

Visit with Boo, Sulley and Mike as you relive your favorite moments from the 2001 Pixar film

*Monster's Inc.* at Monster's Inc., Mike and Sulley to the Rescue.

Travel through the Monster's Inc. plant where you will find Randall Boggs chase Mike and Sulley to get his claws on Boo. Find Boo's door and get her home safe before the Child Detection Agency decontaminates you.

Before you leave, have a short chat with Roz before getting back to the human world.

☐ Have an ice-cold Smoothie at Schmoozies on Hollywood Street

One of the coolest places on Hollywood Street is Schmoozies! Offering your favorite flavors in smoothies along with coffee and juices for every taste.

☐ Visit your favorite Marvel superheroes on Hollywood Street

Marvel superheroes have taken over the area around Hollywood and you now have the chance to meet them during your next visit to Disney California Adventure.

Whether your favorite is Spiderman, Captain America, Black Panther, Thor or Loki, you can get pictures and autographs with them all.

☐ Watch Broadway caliber stage shows at The Hyperion theater

Join the cast of Frozen at this Broadway caliber theater, The Hyperion.

Throughout the history of Disney California Adventure, this theater has played host to Step in Time! And Aladdin, A Musical Spectacular.

Today, relax and enjoy Queen Elsa and Princess Anna, along with their friends Kristoff, Olaf and Sven in the retelling of Frozen live on stage.

☐ Join the dance party with Starlord and Gamora at Guardians of the Galaxy Mission Breakout

Get a front row seat to see your favorite characters from *Guardians of the Galaxy*, Starlord and Gamora as they try to save you all from danger by staging an epic dance off right in front of the new Guardians of the Galaxy: Mission Breakout.

Starlord may even select you to help them dance until the threat has passed.

☐ Get your picture taken with Groot from *Guardians of the Galaxy*

Don't pass up the chance to get your picture taken with your favorite alien tree, Groot at Guardians of the Galaxy: Mission Breakout. At over 7 feet tall, Groot will be the perfect Disney character to pose with for your next souvenir picture.

Be sure to keep an eye out for this favorite character from *Guardians of the Galaxy* at Disney California Adventure.

☐ Explore the collector's room at Guardians of the Galaxy: Mission Breakout

Your experience at Guardians of the Galaxy: Mission Breakout begins when you enter the collector's room. Among the vast collection, you will find many familiar items from the film *Guardians of the Galaxy* and you may even find some items that the collector has taken from the Disney parks themselves.

☐ Find Figment in the collector's warehouse

Figment has lost his way from his home at the Imagination Institute at Epcot and found his way into the collector's warehouse. Can you find him from among the dozens of items on display?

☐ Explore Tivan the Collectors office and find the hidden artifacts

Enter the inner sanctum of Tivan and look around at the shelves of artifacts surrounding you. Among the intergalactic items, you may see some from your favorite Marvel films.

Find the Hydra symbol from *Captain America* and the Hydra helmet from *Captain America: The First Avenger*.

Look through the shelves and find the hat worn by the bell hops of the Hollywood Tower Hotel and book marks within some of the books from this famous hotel that was housed on this very spot.

In addition, you may find a tiny Minnie Mouse figurine hidden amongst the shelves of items.

☐ Learn the language of the Collectors universe

Throughout Guardians of the Galaxy: Mission Breakout, you will find signs in Celestial, the official language of this part of the universe. Guests can learn this language by comparing the letters in Celestial with the letter in English. By the time your ride is finished, you may even be fluent in this intergalactic language.

☐ Find Harold among the items in the collector's warehouse

Hidden somewhere in the collector's warehouse, you will see a collectible that sticks out from among the rest.

High above you on the second floor, you will see a yeti in the corner staring at you from his perch. This guy is known as Harold and he has found his way from the Matterhorn attraction at Disneyland where he lived for decades until he was captured by the collector and brought here for you to see.

Another visitor from Disneyland is nearby Harold on that very same perch. In the darkness, you may see the tentacles of an octopus nearby.

☐ Find the octopus from the Country Bear Jamboree

Dolores the Octopus was a performer at the Country Bear Jamboree in the Vacation Hoedown performing with Terrence the Bear for years before she retired and found her way to the collector's warehouse.

Now she has retired from performing and is another of the collector's captives.

☐ Find the paint covered footprints of Rocket in the queue for Guardians of the Galaxy: Mission Breakout

Rocket has been busy trying to save his friends but, as usual, he is having some fun along the way.

Rocket stumbled on some red paint cans and put his foot in it literally. In the queue on the first floor to the left side, you will see where Rockets has knocked over the red paint and his footprints walking away from the site where the paint is spilled.

- [ ] Ride along with Rocket to save the Guardians of the Galaxy in Mission Breakout

    Get ready to go on an adventure with Rocket and save the Guardians of the Galaxy. Find your way through the collector's abode to help Rocket's friends escape and avoid getting yourself caught.

    You can enjoy this ride with several different soundtracks by your favorite artists so be sure to ride this attraction several time to get rocking with the Guardians of the Galaxy.

- [ ] Find more of the collectors' items in the gift shop for Guardians of the Galaxy: Mission Breakout

    As you exit from your adventure in space, stop to take a look at the cases throughout the gift shop.

    You will find a Light Bright with the words GotG MB, can you decipher the message? Th antique View Master Viewer sitting next to an authentic Spirograph is another of the retro toys lining the walls.

    All your favorite antique toys are displayed in the gift shop so do not miss you favorite before moving on to your next adventure.

*One hundred things you need to do at Disneyland before you die*

☐   Find some more of Rocket's handy work in the gift shop of Guardians of the Galaxy: Mission Breakout

   Rocket has been busy with the sign at the exit of Mission Breakout. As you leave the gift shop, look up at the sign above the doorway. Guests walk under this sign all day without noticing that Rocket has used some more of that red paint to cross out the number and leave his footprints behind.

☐   Find the cargo hold where Rocket escaped from the collector's warehouse

   Outside the attraction for Guardians of the Galaxy: Mission Breakout, you have to look carefully up high on the outside of the building. If you look closely, you will find a cargo hold blown out and Rocket's footprints crawling away from the burned-out area.

☐   Find the Avengers hatch near Guardians of the Galaxy

   Somewhere in the bushes near Guardians of the Galaxy: Mission Breakout, a new neighbor has shown up. The Avenger have put their stamp on this area by installing a hatch with the iconic Avengers symbol emblazoned on the top.

   Take some time to hunt in the plants next to the curb near the entrance to Guardians of the Galaxy to find this secret entrance hatch.

# Grizzly Peak

Come join the campers for some outdoor fun or fly away on a grand adventure at Grizzly Peak when you visit Disney California Adventure. Stop off at Humphrey's to find out what the campers are doing today before soaring through the clouds to visit the wonders of the world.

Stop by the Smokejumper Grill for a burger before you go on your way through Grizzly Peak Airfield.

☐ Read some of the camping notices outside of Humphrey's

To the left of Humphrey's near the soda fountains, you will find glass case with several notices for the campers in the area. Be sure to read the rules and check out the movies being shown in the camp ground during your stay.

Like all of Disneyland resort, you will find little nods to the classic films made famous by Walt Disney.

In this case, find the *Disney's True-Life Adventures*, a series of films showing movie goers the world outside of their neighborhood.

☐ Visit the cash register area of Humphrey's to see some of the camping activities available at Grizzly Peak

Inside Humphrey's, step up to the register and sign up for camping activities. Try your hand a fly fishing, nature hikes or just stargazing if that's your fancy.

Of course, these notices are all for fun, this is yet another example of how Disney's imagineers immerse you in the magic.

☐ Ride on Soarin' Over the World and visit the greatest wonders of the world

Step inside the airplane hangar of Soarin' Around the World as this attraction takes guests on the greatest flight of their lives, traveling to the furthest reaches of their imagination.

Visit the pyramids at Giza, the Taj Mahal in India and the Eiffel Tower in Paris.

Witness the natural wonders of the world like the Matterhorn in Switzerland, the Arctic ocean, Iguazu Falls in Argentina and a herd of elephants in Africa.

End your flight at Disneyland just in time for a spectacular fireworks display.

☐ Stop off at Skyjumpers Grill and read the notes in the shadow boxes

Apart from the amazing food served at Skyjumpers Grill, you will find an amazing array of post cards and notes to Millie thanking her for her amazing cooking and recipes.

Who is Millie, according to the back story of Smyjumpers Grill, she and her husband opened the restaurant and serve the community. Now they serve the guests of Disney California Adventure.

Another fun notice you will find as you enter Smokejumpers Grill. To the left of the entrance, you will find another glass case with a notice from Camp Inch. This is a wonderful nod to the classic *The Parent Trap* starring Haley Mills. She and her sister meet at Camp Inch and trade places to get their parents back together.

☐ Visit the watch tower in front of Soarin' Around the World

Outside of Soarin', guests will notice a large watch tower standing above. This area of Disney California Adventure was designed after the forests of California including the forest ranger tower you see here.

The Mt. Muir lookout is named for geologist John Muir, founder of the Sierra club. This tower offers guests a look at the Sierra Nevada area of California.

☐ Get your picture with the lookout plane

Not far from the entrance to Soarin', you will find a small plane to pose for pictures. While some may be curious why a pane would be placed in this location, Disney added this little plane as a tribute to the brave men and women who patrol the forests in California keeping the wildlife safe from fires.

Take some time to pose for your vacation photos in this picturesque area of Grizzly Peak Airfield.

☐ Visit the Grand California through the Disney California Adventure exit

A little-known entrance to Disney California Adventure can be found just across from the Grizzly River Run attraction. Guests staying at the Grand Californian hotel can enter Disney California Adventure through this entrance during their stay and guests can visit the hotel from Disney California Adventure during theme park hours.

Take some time to explore the exquisite Grand California through this area of Disney California Adventure.

☐ Cool off on a hot day at Grizzly River Run

Another majestic peak in the Disney mountain range is Grizzly Peak at Disney California Adventure. Throughout this mountain are the roaring rapids of California meandering through rock formations with the wildlife and trees offering breathtaking scenery.

Take off on a whirl wind trip down the valley as your boat carries you on a wet ride. Good luck staying dry on this exciting attraction.

☐ Play at the Redwood Creek Challenge Trail

Tucked away from the hustle and bustle of busy life you can go back to nature on the Redwood Creek Challenge Trail.

Greeting you at the entrance are Koda and Kenai from the movie *Brother Bear* as you enter the trail. Find the cargo nets and rope swings throughout this wildlife play area designed specifically for the kids. Little ones can slide down the hollow log or rock climb through the boulders that resemble some of the most beautiful areas of California.

Take some time to see how the rangers who protect our forest live and test some of their equipment as you radio to guests in other parts of the trail.

☐ Find out who your spirit animal is when you touch your hand to the stone at Redwood Creek Challenge Trail

In the furthers reaches of the Redwood Creek Trail you will find a small cave missed by most guests.

Within this cave, press your hand to the cave wall and suddenly the cave comes to life to reveal your spirit animal, the animal whose spirit will guide your life to your purpose. Don't miss this small reminder of the Disney film *Brother Bear* as you enjoy this quiet part of Disney California Adventure.

☐ Wander the back trail of Grizzly Peak

A little know trail through Grizzly Peak stands on the back side of the Grizzly River Run attraction. A quiet pathway through this area, guests can enjoy a roaring waterfall and picturesque scenery allowing for a reprive from the hectic day.

Be sure to find this little treasure through Grizzly Peak on your next trip through Disney California Adventure.

# Cars land

Walk down the street of your favorite Pixar film, *Cars*. Radiator Spring welcomes you as you get a room at the Cozy Cone motel or get a new paint job at Ramone's.

Grab a bite to eat at Flo's V-8 Café or grab a conecoction at the Cozy Cone. Meet your favorite Pixar friends Lightening McQueen and Mater right on the street.

Ride along with Mater on his Junkyard Jamboree or race through Route 66 on your way to the Piston Cup on Radiator Spring Racers.

☐ Get your picture taken in front of the Cars Land sign at the entrance to Radiator Springs

> Stop and get your photograph taken at the sign for Cars Land. This billboard shows the sites of Radiator Springs and you are the star of the picture. The perfect souvenir of your time at Radiator Springs is

waiting for you at the entrance to this enchanting little town.

☐ Ride your own tractor in Mater's Junkyard Jamboree

Join the Jamboree as you swing with the tractors round and round the dancefloor with Mater calling the dance for you.

Mater's Junkyard holds clues to Mater's other professions as you see his private eye sign or Mater the daredevil while you are waiting for your turn at the dancefloor.

☐ Get your picture taken with a baby tractor

The junkyard hosts full grown tractors for you to ride but there is a special little tractor just waiting in the petting zoo for guests to pose for pictures with this little guy.

☐ Get a cool drink at Filmore's

Radiator Springs favorite hippy offers the best in organic juices at Filmore's. For the humans looking for something cool, stop to get a soda or water for the trip down this long road.

☐ Visit Sarge's Surplus Hut to see the latest in military surplus

Sarge may be retired from his duty to the country he loves but he brings some of that love to Radiator Springs when he opened Sarge's Surplus Hut.

While visiting Sarge's be sure to see the miniature Radiator Springs or take one home for your very own.

☐ Spend the night at the Cozy Cone Motel in Radiator Springs or just have a bite to eat in the concoctions

Sally Carrera has set up the Cozy Cone motel for weary travels to stop and freshen up before continuing on their journey through Radiator Springs.

Stop for a rest and pick up some Pop cone, Ice cream cone, Conecoctions or a Churro.

While you are there be sure to peek in the registration office to see post cards and knick knacks from Radiator Springs.

☐ Find Buzz Lightyear hiding in the registration area of the Cozy Cone Motel

> Hiding inside the Cozy Cone registration office you will find another friend from Pixar hiding amongst the road cone souvenirs.
>
> Buzz Lightyear stopped by and is trying to get back to Andy as he sneaks through the office to find his way home.
>
> Look around at the small orange road cones on the side of the registration desk to find this fun little Easter egg.

☐ Grab a bite to eat at Flo's V-8 Drive in

> Get refueled with some tasty treats from Flo's V-8 Café.
>
> Gets some high-octane munchies or a delicious shake in this road side café.

☐ Sit in the Clinic and see some of Doc Hudson's trophy's

> Doc Hudson has set up his doctor's office right next door to Flo's to help the residents of Radiator Springs stay heathy.

Take a look at his x-rays or his many degrees or sneak around the garage to see his previous life as a racecar with his Piston Cups and newspaper clippings.

- [ ] Stop in at Ramone's for a new paint job

    Ramone keeps the visitors looking great as you shop for the latest in Radiator Sprigs wear.

    During Halloween, stop in Ramones to see his Día De Los Muertos altar and do not miss Christmas at Ramones where you will find all of your gifts for the special cars in your life.

- [ ] Visit Luigi's Rollickin' Roadsters to see the premium tires in Radiator Springs

    For the best in tires, you can not beat Luigi's showroom. When you are done shopping for your new tires, take some time to stop in the lot behind Luigi's to visit with Luigi's cousins from Italy and dance along with them to the strains of songs from their homeland.

    Whirl and twirl with the Rollickin' Roadsters as they show you what they have learned at Luigi's.

☐ Get your picture with Radiator Springs founder Stanley when you visit his statue

The founder of Radiator Spring waits for you to get your picture with him in front of the firehouse.

Stanley, complete with his gold tooth, stand in the exact spot where Radiator Springs was founded near a natural spring. Searching for his fortune, Stanley stopped here to fill his radiator and stayed to build the town you see.

☐ Find the 8 ¾ wonder of the world in the queue for Radiator Springs Racers

As you enter the queue for Radiator Springs Racers and wind your way through, stop at the namesake of the town of Radiator Springs.

Here you will find the 8 ¾ wonder of the world founded by Stanley, the town patriarch. Make a wish and throw a coin in this natural wonder to make your dreams come true.

☐ Get in your car and get sidetracked on your way to the Piston Cup on Radiator Springs Racers

Travel along ornament valley as you explore the valley around Radiator Springs.

Go tractor tipping with Mater or race along the ridge of the canyon before stopping to get a new set of tires or a new paint job before the big race.

Doc Hudson coaches you as you take off on a high-speed race through the valley to see who wins the race.

☐ Meet your favorite cars Mater and Lightening McQueen in front of the Cozy Cone Motel

Your favorite racer Lightening McQueen and his best friend Mater are taking time off of their busy schedule to meet guests visiting the sleepy town of Radiator Springs. Get your camera ready to get pictures with these celebrities when they hang out in front of the Cozy Cone Motel to greet you.

Be sure to stop by during the holidays as Lightening McQueen and Mater don their Halloween costumes or Holiday best.

# Pacific Wharf

Visit the seaside village of California at Pacific Wharf. Enjoy some of the local cuisine as you dine al fresco with a refreshing margarita or craft beer. For those looking for something sweet, visit Ghirardelli for an ice cream.

- [ ] Visit the Walt Disney Imagineering Blue Sky Cellar

    The Disneyland resort is constantly changing and the Walt Disney Imagineering Blue Sky Cellar shows guests the newest areas being developed for future attraction.

    Be first to see the designs, sketches and models for the newest innovations coming in the future. Guests will be amazed at the new attractions coming to life from the minds of the imagineers at Disneyland resort.

☐ Join the bakery tour at Boudin's Bakery

A mainstay of the San Francisco area is the Boudin sourdough bread and now you can have the taste of the Boudin family bakery at Disney California Adventure.

Stop in and witness first hand how the bakers take the bread from starter to finished product while enjoying a taste of this delicious bread during your tour.

Then stop in next door and buy a loaf to take home to continue enjoying this treat for days to come.

☐ Indulge your sweet tooth at Ghirardelli Soda Fountain and Chocolate Shop

The name Ghirardelli is synonymous with rich chocolate and this famous chocolatier has brought these treats to Disney California Adventure.

Sample the original chocolates or dive into one of the signature sundae's as you sit outside and enjoy the California sunshine.

☐ Enjoy your favorite food at Pacific Wharf

Whether you enjoy Chinese or Mexican cuisine, be sure to stop at Pacific Wharf to find your favorites.

The Lucky Fortune Cookery offers stir fry favorites direct from China town in San Francisco while Cocina Cucamonga offers flavors from south of the boarder.

Along side these options are soups and salads in authentic sour dough bread bowls at Pacific Wharf Café.

Whether you are looking for a meal or a snack look no further than Pacific Wharf to find your favorite.

☐ Enjoy a frozen cocktail at Rita's Baja Blenders

For those looking for adult beverages, Rita's Baja Blenders offers both margarita's and non-alcoholic options for younger guests.

Enjoy the lemon lime or strawberry margarita to cool off on a warm day or a red sangria to enjoy a wine option.

☐ Enjoy a Karl Strauss beverage at Pacific Wharf Distribution Co.

For adults looking for something cool, head over to the Pacific Wharf Distribution truck at Pacific Wharf for a cold Karl Strauss beer. These hand-crafted beers offer a variety of flavors to choose from.

Check out the Karl Strauss truck next time you are on Pacific Wharf.

- [ ] Enjoy a unique vintage at Alfresco tasting Terrace

    These Italian inspired wines offer guests a fresh taste on their favorite wines. Enjoy the outdoor terrace as you watch Radiator Springs across the way. Join your friends for a bottle or wine flight next time you are at Disney California Adventure.

- [ ] Enjoy a meal and adult beverage at Sonoma Terrace

    Sonoma Terrace offers a variety for snacks along with hand crafted beer and wine for guests looking for something unique.

    Enjoy Bavarian pretzels or flat bread pizza with a wine or beer to perfectly compliment these yummy treats.

    Enjoy the view of the lake and Pixar Pier as you indulge your tastes in this charming atmosphere.

# Paradise Garden Park

Along the lake, guests will find Paradise Garden Park where attractions meet the water's edge.

☐ Ride in a clam shell to go under the sea with The Little Mermaid: Ariel's Undersea Adventures

   Climb aboard a clamshell that will take you down into the depths of the ocean as you relive the story with Ariel and her friends Scuttle, Sebastien and Flounder.

   Watch out for Ursula and her eels along your journey and celebrate with the rest of King Triton's subjects at the marriage of Ariel ad Eric.

☐ Find the incredible Mr. Limpet in The Little Mermaid: Ariel's Undersea Adventures

One of the guests celebrating along with Sebastien in Under the Sea is the fish from the film The Incredible Mr. Limpet.

Find Mr. Limpet across from Ariel as she dances to the music in this party scene. He is wearing his signature glasses and peeking from the plants.

☐ Enjoy a corndog at Corndog Castle

For those looking for something to fill them up while exploring Paradise Garden Park, stop at Corndog Castle

This themed food stand offers guests the famed Disney corndog so be sure to stop by on your next adventure through Disney California Adventure.

☐ Become a pilot at Goofy's Sky School

Learn to fly along with Goofy as you take his 4 step lessons to become a pilot.

Soar with the birds as you fly up and down along the track. Hold on to your hat as you take the turns or take the dips towards the finish line.

*One hundred things you need to do at Disneyland before you die*

☐ Ride Jumpin' Jellyfish

Climb aboard your own jellyfish and ride among the kelp as you go up and down in this ride designed for the little ones in your party. This colorful ride is a joy for the kids as they experience what it feels like to bounce among the waves.

☐ Become part of the action on The Band Concert swings

Join Mickey Mouse and all his friends while they play inside the tornado in this ride based on the 1935 short subject *The Band Concert*. Conductor Mickey Mouse stands high above while his orchestra spins in the cyclone while not missing a note.

Get caught up in the wind in your own swing as you join in the fun.

☐ Go back in time to ride on the Golden Zephyr

For fans of Buck Rogers, a ride on the Golden Zephyr is like a ride on a space ship from the 1950's. Travel above the lake and see the sights of California Adventure on this throwback to the science fiction of the 1950's.

- [ ] Enjoy a hearty lunch at Boardwalk Pizza and Pasta or Paradise Garden Grill

    Tucked back along the Boardwalk is an area that offers guests several food options that will tempt your tastebuds.

    Try your favorite pizza or pasta at Boardwalk Pizza and Pasta or Paradise Garden Grill for healthier options. Be sure to stop for a great meal and relax in this garden setting.

- [ ] Listen to live music during your meal at Paradise Garden Grill

    Throughout the year, Paradise Garden offers live musical acts in this al fresco dining area. Listen to music from all over the globe while you enjoy your meal.

# Pixar Pier

Disney California Adventure shows guests the best of the Pixar films in this new area Pixar Pier. Now you can experience *The Incredibles*, *Toy Story* and *Up* while surrounding by the calming water neaby.

Stroll along the boardwalk and stop for an ice-cold drink while taking in the enchantment of this adorable area. Grab an ice cream or turkey leg to keep you going before riding the thrilling Incredicoaster. Play with your friends from Toy Story on Toy Story Mania and get your picture with your favorite toys.

Play some games of chance along the boardwalk or stop into the shops to get the latest in Pixar style.

- ☐ Have cocktails overlooking the lake at Lamplight Lounge

    Stop for a cool drink on a warm day on the boardwalk.

Whether it's a themed libation or snacks before heading to another exciting attraction, you won't want to miss this hot spot at the top of Pixar Pier.

☐ Get your new favorite souvenir at Knick Knacks

Everyone's favorite little snow globe has now opened his own shop on Pixar Pier. Stop in and check out the latest in Pixar merchandise to pick the perfect memento of your time at Pixar Pier.

Do not miss a chance to see Disney artists sketching one of a kind characters right before your eyes and check out the story boards of your favorite films around the store.

☐ Get a soft serve ice cream at the Adorable Snowman Frosted Treats

A cool treat on a hot day, Paradise Pier offers the best ice cream around. Taste the classic vanilla, velvety smooth lemon or a blueberry lemon parfait.

The Adorable Snowman has been busy getting these treats ready for hungry guests but do not worry, its lemon.

☐ Explore the billboard messages on Pixar Pier

The Pixar characters are lending their fame to speak to guests about having fun with billboards on Pixar

Pier. Enjoy these clever messages that show the gang from Finding Dory asking for help keeping the Pier clean and the Coco family telling guests to enjoy these moments.

Get family photos in front of the lovely works of art before continuing your adventures on Pixar Pier.

☐ Listen for Dash at the beginning of the Incredicoaster

If you stand on the pier above the launch area of the Incredicoaster, listen carefully and you will hear Dash count down to the launch of this high-speed coaster.

Dash can be heard revving up his feet to send the Incredicoaster on its way. Be sure to listen as he counts down to this thrilling attraction.

☐ Ride the Incredicoaster with The Incredibles

Mr. Incredible, Elastigirl, Dash, Violet and Jack Jack greet you as you take off on a high-speed adventure with this famous family.

Hold on as you travel through the inverted loop and soar over the streets of Pixar on this incredible ride. Help the incredibles find Jack Jack as he uses all of his powers along the way.

- [ ] Meet the characters from The Incredibles

    Meet Mr. and Mrs. Incredible along with their children and friends Frozone and Edna Mode in the area around the Incredicoaster every day. The Incredibles love greeting guests and posing for pictures. Be on the lookout for Frozone or Edna Mode as they joins their friends to greet the guests braving their newest attraction.

- [ ] Have a cookie at Jack Jack's

    Step up to the counter of Jack Jack's and try his favorite snack, cookies. The chocolate chip offers thick chocolate throughout this huge cookie. Enjoy your favorite sweets at Jack Jack's.

- [ ] Find your favorite critter on Jessie's Critter Carousel

    Join Jessie and all her desert friends as you hop aboard Jessie's Critter Carousel and take a ride

    Great fun for the whole family, the critters welcome you to join in the fun with good old western tunes.

- [ ] Find the Emperor Zurg toy at Poultry Palace

    Poultry Palace offers snacks to guests during their time at Pixar Pier but few notice the tiny Emperor Zurg toy that comes with the meal box that houses this food stand.

You can find Zurg on the roof of the box or nearby so be sure to get a picture with this adorable version of Emporer Zurg.

☐ Spend some time with Mr. Potato Head as you wait for your ride on Toy Story Mania

Mr. Potato Head is waiting to entertain you by telling jokes, singing and interacting with the guests as you wait in line. Find out about some of his friends as he makes sport of them, listen to his song stylings or just talk to him as he asks questions of the guests.

Visit your favorite Toy Story characters in front of Toy Story Mania

Throughout the day, you will find Woody, Buzz and Bo Peep taking pictures and signing autographs for guests in the area in front of Toy Story Mania.

Get your autograph book and camera ready for this great souvenir of your day on Pixar Pier.

☐ Play this twist on classic carnival games on Toy Story Mania

Join Hamm, Trixie, the aliens and green army men as you try your skill in four different carnival games. Pop the balloons, knock the targets down, toss the rings and shoot darts to raise your score.

As your game comes to an end, check your score against others in your ride vehicle and find out how far up the scale you get. Keep pulling the string and watch confetti celebrate your score.

☐ Try a hot dog at Angry Dogs

Try the spicy Angry Dog or a more traditional hot dog as you work your way around Pixar Pier. Enjoy chips and a drink to round out your snack with Anger from *Inside Out*.

☐ Enjoy a flavored churro at Senior Buzz Churros

Buzz Lightyear has been reset once again and now is making traditional churros for guests of Pixar Pier.

Enjoy the Spicy churro or a cinnamon sugar churro for those looking for something more traditional.

☐ Play for favorite carnival games

Join Bullseye, Heimlich, Walle and the cast of La Luna as you play traditional carnival games for adorable prizes.

Race along with Bullseye against your friends or blast Eve high into the sky to win fun plush prizes.

Throw the candy corn into the basket with Heimlich or hook onto the stars to try your skills by yourself.

Whether young or old, do not miss a game of chance on Pixar Pier.

☐ Ride on the swinging cars on the Pixar Pal-A-Round

Find your favorite Pixar character and ride with them on the swinging cars of Pixar's Pal-A-Round. Get a bird's eye view of the Pixar Pier and the lake as you relax on this classic attraction with colorful cars and the adorable Pixar characters adorning each ride car.

Enjoy this relaxing lakeside attraction at Pixar Pier.

☐ Visit Bing Bong's Sweet Stuff

The best of both worlds come together at Bing Bong's Sweet Stuff where you can get the best of candy and baked good on one side or your favorite Pixar themed merchandise on the opposite. High in the middle stands Bing Bong riding his rocket ship wagon and crying candy.

Be sure to stop into Bing Bong's Sweet Stuff on your next vacation to see Riley's imaginary friend for yourself.

☐ Ride with Joy and Sadness on Inside Out Emotional Whirlwind

Ride high above Pixar Pier with all of the emotions on Inside Out Emotional Whirlwind. Get your picture taken with Sadness or Fear before getting in line for this charming ride that brings you face to face with your emotions.

Ride along with Joy, Sadness, Fear, Disgust and Anger along with Bing Bong and rainbow unicorn as you go around and around before coming back to earth.

# Halloween

Halloween at Disney California Adventure is a feast for the eyes as guests immerse themselves in the sights and sounds of Halloween throughout the park.

☐ Get pictures and video of Oogie Boogie talking to guests in the Esplanade of Disney California Adventure

During the Halloween season, Oogie Boogie sits atop the entrance taunting guests to enter the parks. Be sure to get picture with this *Nightmare Before Christmas* villain and get video of his tormenting laughter before entering Disney California Adventure.

☐ Get your picture with the Headless Horseman statue

Featured in front of the shops along Buena Vista Street, take a moment to pose with the statue of the infamous headless horseman. Surprises await through who are brave enough to be seen with this legendary figure of literature as you might see hidden figures within the PhotoPass.

- [ ] Get your picture taken with Mickey, Donald, Goofy and Minnie dressed up for Halloween

    Come face to face with a ghost, a devil, a witch or a sorcerer as your friends pose for picture this Halloween.

    You just might recognize these costumed figures as your friends Mickey, Minnie, Donald, Daisy and Goofy.

    Don't miss this opportunity for a picture this Halloween.

- [ ] Get your picture with the Cars Land Haul O Ween sign at the entrance to Radiator Springs.

    Stop at the classic Cars Land billboard dressed for Haul O Ween as you immortalize your visiting to Radiator Springs during this festive time of year.

    Do not miss a picture with a tiny witch sitting alongside this billboard.

☐ See how the residents of Cars Land decorate for Halloween

Walk the main street of Radiator Springs as you see the residents decorate for this spooky time of year.

Get your photo with the spider car in front of Flo's V-8, find the tire chain spider webs, pose for pictures in front of the cornucopia or pose with the Cozy Cone Jack O Lanterns.

Find the gas can pumpkin patch or pose with founder Stanley in front of the spooky fire station.

☐ Ride Mater's Graveyard JamBooree

Mater has been busy getting his junkyard ready for Halloween and changing the music to match the haunted feel of Radiator Springs.

Join his tractor dancers for a wild ride around the junk yard this Halloween during the Junkyard JamBooree.

☐ Get a picture with the baby tractor dressed for Halloween

In the petting zoo of Mater's Junkyard JamBooree you will find the cutest little tractor waiting for picture in her mummy costume.

Be sure to get your Halloween picture with this little cutie next time you visit Mater's during Halloween.

☐ Peek in the office of the Cozy Cone Motel to see a special Halloween surprise

The Cozy Cone has gotten into the spirit of Halloween with the office decorated with oil splatter on the windows and on the floor. Take a close look at the Cozy Cone and see the small model of the Brakes Motel, the Cars Land take on the movie *Psycho*.

☐ Get your picture with Lightening McQueen or Mater in their Halloween costumes

Join Lightening McQueen as he dresses up for Halloween as his favorite super hero. Mater gets his spooky on as Count Dracula. If your lucky, you will even find the fire truck dresses as a clown.

☐ Ride on Luigi's Honkin' Haul-O-Ween

Luigi's is joining in the Halloween fun when he changes the party to Luigi's Honkin' Haul-O-Ween. These adorable tire salesmen have decked out the showroom with tire tread pumpkins and spooky songs playing with cars dancing beneath the candy corn colored flags.

Be sure to stop at Luigi's this Halloween.

☐ Find the fall Cornucopia

> Just outside Luigi's you can find the fall cornucopia filled with Cars Land versions of fall favorites. Gas can Jack O'Lanterns, oil can corn and tail light flowers adorn the horn of plenty in this festive picture spot.

☐ Find the Día De Los Muertos display in Ramones

> Stop into Ramones and see his Mexican heritage on full display as the altar for Día De Los Muertos demonstrates the remembrance of his dead relatives. If you look closely, you will recognize the memorial to Doc Hudson who has passed on.

☐ Pose for a picture with the paper mâché Día De Los Muertos car

> Outside of Ramones store, be sure to stop for a picture with this brightly decorated paper mâché car to celebrate this Mexican tradition.

☐ Ride Guardians of the Galaxy: Monsters after Dark

> The Guardians of the Galaxy have lost Groot somewhere in the Collectors warehouse and it is up to you to help them find him. Beware, since the monsters have been let out of their cages and they are after you.

☐ Watch the Musical Celebration of Coco

> Join Miguel and his family as they celebrate the Día De Los Muertos at Disney California Adventure. These life size marionettes retell the story of *Coco* as they sing and dance to your favorite songs from this enchanting film.
>
> Enjoy the classic Folklorico dance troupe as they celebrate along with Miguel as he plays his father's guitar.

☐ Honor your loved ones in the Plaza De La Familia

> Visit the Plaza De La Familia and join in the honored traditions that define Dia De Los Muertos. Write the name of your loved one on one of the cards and tie it to the chains on the wall of memories. Marvel at the marigolds that decorate this area and the life size skeleton figures that have been lovingly created for this festival.

☐ Visit the alter to Ernesto De La Cruz

> Miguel has been busy creating an altar to his favorite musician, Ernesto De La Cruz. Hundreds of candles and personal items that define the life of De La Cruz surround the area along with record albums and posters of this famous Mariachi.

This area also shows the animation that went into the film *Coco*. Spend some time in the world of this new Disney classic.

☐ Sample the flavors of Mexico at Paradise Garden Grill

Enjoy the distinctive flavors of Mexico at Paradise Garden Grill during the Halloween season. Tacos and Tamales offer savory fillings and wash it down with a Mexican hot chocolate.

Give your taste buds a treat with these delectable offerings at Paradise Garden Grill.

# Christmas at Disney California Adventure

Join in the holiday fun in a very special way at Disney California Adventure. Get special Christmas treats or pictures with your favorite characters as you celebrate the holiday in your own unique way.

Visit the streets of Hollywood to see the glitz of the shiny garland or visit with your friends at Radiator Springs. Whatever your choices of traditions, you will find it at Disney California Adventure.

☐ Get pictures with the Christmas tree at the end of Buena Vista Street

> This beautifully decorated Christmas tree is adorned with ornaments from the 1920's and 1930's for your viewing pleasure. Do not miss out on a picture with this stunning tree for your scrapbook.
>
> Join in the tree lighting ceremony each evening as this spectacular tree comes to life with twinkling

lights and glowing ornaments decorating this fabulous fifty-foot tree.

☐ Get a holiday treat at Trolley Treats.

Just in time for the holidays you will find specially decorated candy apples, fudge and various holiday themed sweets. Find your favorite as you peruse the cases of Trolley Treats.

Be sure to get your own hand crooked candy cane made by the candy artisans at Disney California Adventure.

☐ Walk down Hollywood street to see the glittering decorations.

As you wander down Hollywood Street, your eyes will be dazzled at the shiny tinsel garland that is wrapped around the lamp posts and the pictures of Santa Claus adorning the sidewalks. At the end of Hollywood Street, you will find Santa Claus and his reindeer flying through the air next to the Hyperion Theater.

☐ Visit the Cars Land billboard to get a picture with this icon.

Get your Seasons Speedings at the Cars Land billboard that has been transformed for the holidays.

The billboard offers guests an amazing backdrop for Holiday pictures.

☐ Pose for a picture with the Cars Land snowman.

Near the Cars Land billboard, find this adorable Cars snowman with his road cone nose and shiny hubcaps. This little guy will be front and center of your Christmas picture from Disney California Adventure.

☐ Visit the streets of Radiator Springs to see the décor

White wall wreaths and air filter garland adorn the streets of Radiator Springs. Find the Christmas tree decorated with shiny hubcaps and pose for a picture with Founder Stanley in his bronze Santa hat and bag of goodies.

The residents of Radiator Springs have been hard at work decorating every inch of Route 66 so spend some time admiring their décor this Christmas season.

☐ Ride Mater's Jingle Jamboree

Mater is feeling the holiday season as he dresses his Junkyard Jamboree for Christmas. Jump in your tractor and listen to the Cars version of your favorite Christmas songs like Deck the Halls, The Dreidel Song and his classic Junkyard Jamboree.

- [ ] Visit Sarge's to see his salute to America Christmas lights

    Only Sarge can deck the halls with an American flag as inspiration. Visit with Sarge and see the hundreds of lights on his store and in the trees to get in the Christmas mood.

- [ ] Find the Route 66 Christmas tree on the streets of Radiator Springs

    Radiator Springs gets in the spirit while honoring the famous Route 66. Find the Christmas tree near the Cozy Cone Motel and get your picture with this adorable decoration.

- [ ] Visit the Cozy Cone Motel to see the holiday décor

    The road cone Christmas trees are scattered throughout the grounds of the Cozy Cone Motel. Be sure to visit the office to catch a glimpse of the Cozy Cone gingerbread house before moving on down the road.

- [ ] Ride Luigi's Joy to the Whirl ride

    Join Luigi and all his cousins in this Christmastime dance. Listen to the Christmas tunes as you rock from side to side and spin through the dancefloor. Be sure to take pictures in the tire showroom before your ride begins.

- [ ] Visit Flo's V-8 to see her spin on Christmas

    Join Flo for bite to eat and get a load of her shiny Christmas trees with her hit records decorating them. Take a close look to see the labels of her favorite records throughout the café.

- [ ] Visit the Christmas trees throughout California Adventure.

    Throughout Disney California Adventure, you will find the sights of Christmas with trees throughout the park. Visit Pixar Pier or the area in front of The Light Mermaid attraction to find trees decorated to perfection to get you in the Christmas spirit.

- [ ] Celebrate the holidays with the countries of the world at Festival of Holidays

    Countries throughout the world celebrate in their very unique way and now Disney California Adventure brings these traditions to guests during the Festival of Holidays.

    Dancers, musicians and artists from every corner of the globe converge to show guests their talents and make you a part of the love felt at this holiday season.

*One hundred things you need to do at Disneyland before you die*

I hope you have enjoyed this peek into the Disneyland resort. Whether this is your first visit or you are a regular visitor, The Ultimate Disneyland Bucket List can be your constant companion to discover new delights at these iconic theme parks.

www.ingramcontent.com/pod-product-compliance
Lightning Source LLC
Chambersburg PA
CBHW071339080526
44587CB00017B/2892